AN EARLY VILLAGE SITE

AT ZAWI CHEMI SHANIDAR

UNDENA PUBLICATIONS

MALIBU 1981

Bibliotheca Mesopotamica

Primary sources and interpretive analyses for the study of Mesopotamian civilization and its influences from late prehistory to the end of the cuneiform tradition

Edited by Giorgio Buccellati

Volume Thirteen

Published Under the Auspices of
IIMAS
The International Institute for Mesopotamian Area Studies

An Early Village Site At Zawi Chemi Shanidar

by Rose L. Solecki

Undena Publications
Malibu 1980

The early village site at Zawi Chemi Shanidar, located in Shanidar Valley in the Zagros Mountains of northern Iraq, dates from the ninth millenium B.C., a time when such open settlements were being established in favored locations in Southwestern Asia. During this early Post-Pleistocene period important cultural changes were taking place in the region, and the Zawi Chemi village site reflects these new subsistence stratiegies and technological processes. Plant food was processed in sizable amounts on the basis of abundant milling equipment, and a study of the animal bones suggests that sheep were being kept by the end of the Zawi Chemi occupation, although hunting was still important. The rich Zawi Chemi cultural inventory represents both terminal Palaeolithic and early Neolithic traditions. It was in fact a period of much experimentation, and what most characterizes Zawi Chemi material culture is the variety of the tools and the technological and even artistic innovations present in it.

This report is a study of the site of Zawi Chemi Shanidar with an emphasis on the early Zawi Chemi village, although a later occupation dating after the sixth century A.D. is also discussed. The culture of Zawi Chemi village is fully described and interpreted; its relationships to both local and regional enviromental settings discussed; comparisons are made with roughly contemporary sites in Southwestern Asia (e.g. Karim Shahir and Natufian); and finally there is a cultural and ecological overview.

Library of Congress Card Number 80-54671

ISBN 0-89003-068-5 (softbound)

0-89003-067-7 (hardbound)

Undena Publications, P.O.Box 97, Malibu, CA 90265, U.S.A.

FOREWORD

Many persons have contributed to this study of the site of Zawi Chemi Shanidar, and I wish to thank them here at the beginning of this report. First, I wish to thank the State Organization of Antiquities of Iraq who made all the official arrangements necessary for our work at Shanidar. Furthermore, I wish to personally thank the following government representatives who were with us during the 1956-1957 and 1960 seasons when the excavations at Zawi Chemi Shanidar took place: Sabri Shukri, Tariq Madhloom, and Ibrahim el Zayri. I also wish to mention and to thank my three colleagues and friends, George Maranjian, Philip E. L. Smith, and Jacques Bordaz, each of whom spent some time in excavation at the site. In addition, I must thank Arlette Leroi-Gourhan for her important palynological study (Appendix III); Isabella Milling Drew for her study of metallurgy from Layer A at Zawi Chemi Shanidar (Appendix II); and Nancy M. Waggoner for her valuable assistance in the identification of a coin found in Layer A at the site (Appendix I).

Lastly, I want to thank my husband, Ralph S. Solecki, who originally located the site of Zawi Chemi Shanidar, and who has encouraged and aided me throughout the preparation of this report.

The investigations at Zawi Chemi Shanidar as part of the larger Shanidar project were financed under grants from the Smithsonian Institution, the American Philosophical Society, the Wenner-Gren Foundation for Anthropological Research, Columbia University, and the National Science Foundation.

TABLE OF CONTENTS

LIST OF FIGURES

LIST OF PLATES

LIST OF TABLES

CHAPTER 1

INTRODUCTION

The early village site of Zawi Chemi Shanidar (R.L. Solecki, 1964, 1972, 1977; R.L. Solecki and R.S. Solecki, 1963, 1970) is located in Shanidar valley, in the rugged Zagros mountains of northern Iraq. It is situated on the first prominent terrace of the left bank of the Greater Zab river, a branch of the Tigris (pl. 1, figs. 1,2). Although it is surrounded by high mountains over 1800 meters high, the site itself has an elevation of only about 425 meters. The site lies in a modern wheat field, adjacent to a permanent spring and the small Kurdish village of Shanidar. The local site name, Zawi Chemi Daraw Shanidar (which we have shortened to Zawi Chemi Shanidar) in Kurdish means "the field by the gulley of Shanidar." At the present time the surface of the field is strewn with stones, many of which are pieces of ancient tools. On the basis of these surface finds the site extends over an area approximately 250x275 meters. There is no mound or other topographic feature to indicate the presence of an ancient living site. Zawi Chemi Shanidar is about four kilometers from Shanidar cave (R.S. Solecki, 1955) as the crow flies, or within a good hour's walking distance.

Zawi Chemi Shanidar was excavated during two field seasons: 1956-1957 and 1960. The site was tested (Tests 1 and 2) in November 1956 and then a major cut (Cut 1) was excavated in the spring of 1957. This cut was enlarged during the summer of 1960 (Cut 2). In all, an area of 112 square meters was excavated in part to a depth of three meters.

CHAPTER 2

EXCAVATIONS

Test 1 (fig. 1) was laid out in an area that had a concentration of surface finds. Test 2 (fig. 1) was placed fifty meters to the south, to investigate the area closer to the river. Cut 1 (fig. 1) was laid out around Test 1 to further outline the stone structure uncovered there. Cut 2 (fig. 1) was laid out directly to the northeast of Cut 1.

The areas to be investigated were first scraped to clear away surface debris, and then the excavations were made in arbitrary 20 or 25 cm. levels. The first 50 cm. were not screened, but all lower deposits were screened when possible. It was not always possible to screen the deposits of Cut 1 due to the almost daily rains which fell during the excavation. Cut 2, however, was completely screened below the 50 cm. level; in fact all this material was checked through twice to ensure maximum recovery of the microlithic sized pieces.

Test 1 (figs. 1,3) measured 8.0x1.0 m. and was laid out in a northeast-southwest direction, approximately 100 m. from the banks of the Greater Zab river and 125 m. west of the gulley in which Shanidar spring was located. The trench was excavated in arbitrary 20 cm. levels, through cultural deposits to a depth of two meters. Test 2 (fig. 1) measured only 2.0x3.0 m., and was placed between Test 1 and the river. It proved to have a shallow, culturally mixed deposit, at most only 50 cm. deep, above a gravel layer. Cut 1 (figs. 1,3) was laid out 12.0x10.0 m., as an enlargement of Test 1. The southeast wall of the C row of Cut 1 coincided with the southeast wall of Test 1 (see fig. 3). Due to the lack of time and bad weather only part of Cut 1, an area 6.0x8.0 m., was excavated to native soil (fig. 3). Cut 2 (figs. 1,3) was laid out, 8.0x8.0 m., directly to the northeast of Cut 1. The former was at a slightly higher elevation than the latter because the land slopes up from the river. There was also a gap of some centimeters between the two cuts because of erosion on the exposed northeast face of Cut 1, during the three year hiatus in excavation. The dumps for Test 1 and Cut 1 were located on the site of Cut 2, so they had to be moved and the surface scraped prior to the excavation of Cut 2. Also a modern stone wall, a field marker, had to be removed from the area of Cut 2.

CHAPTER 3

STRATIGRAPHY

There are two distinct cultural occupations at Zawi Chemi Shanidar: a late one (Layer A) which dates no earlier than the sixth century A.D., on the basis of an associated Byzantine coin (pl. 2j, Appendix I), and a Proto-Neolithic layer (Layer B) which dates from 10,870±300 years ago on the basis of carbon-14 dating (Solecki and Rubin, 1958, p. 1446). This Proto-Neolithic layer, which refers to the Zawi Chemi cultural horizon, is the prime concern of the present paper. Layer A materials were concentrated in the first 50 cm. of the deposits, but they also occurred below because the later people disturbed some of the earlier deposits. At the same time early materials have worked their way up into the late deposits, and as already noted can be found on the surface of the site today.

3.1. Layer A

Layer A had a maximum depth of about 60 cm., and consisted of two roughly horizontal natural layers (figs. 4-6): an upper, plow torn, black colored one and immediately below that a brown earth layer with vertical black streaks from the top layer. Mixed in the deposits were areas of charcoal and reddened burned earth, and large and small stones. There were broad gravel lenses, ca. 10 cm. thick, in the southwestern part of Cut 1 (the part closest to the river) from about 30 to 50 cm. below datum.

The Layer A cultural inventory indicates a relatively recent date for the occupation. There is much pottery, the most diagnostic of which is the so-called "Christian Ware," (pl. 2c-f) so named because of the characteristic cross figures stamped on it (Campbell Thompson and Mallowan, 1933). There are also metal tools (pl. 2g-i), bits of old glass, and other obviously recent objects.

Six large pits attributable to the Layer A people were uncovered during the excavations (pl. 2a,b). These were dug in part through their own refuse and in part down into Layer B. Three are located in Cut 1 and three in Cut 2. The three in Cut 1 run in an east-west direction and are roughly a meter and a half to somewhat over two meters apart. Pit A, located in square C2, is flat bottomed and measured 72 cm. in diameter and was 80 cm. deep. It was filled with dark earth mixed with stones, charcoal bits, and burned earth fragments. Found in the pit area was a copper or bronze needle (pl. 2i), pottery, a bone tool, and flint flakes. Pit B, located partly in square B3 and partly in unexcavated square A3, was first noticed in the 25-50 cm. level and continued down to slightly below the 90 cm. level. It measured about 110 cm. in diameter. It was filled with dark earth and many rocks, and contained much pottery, a copper coin (pl. 2j, Appendix I), an iron spear point (pl. 2g), an iron ball, a piece of slag, a glass fragment, a bone tool and a muller fragment. Pit C (pl. 2a,b) was a flat bottomed pit, located in square D1 to the east of Pit A. It was first noticed in the 25-50 cm. level, and had its base at 85 cm. It was filled with dark earth, large and small stones, much pottery (from two vessels), and animal bones. There was also a piece of wire which was probably modern because it showed no signs of corrosion.

Three pits were found in Cut 2, again oriented in a row, but this time running northeast-southwest. The structure of at least two of these pits, however, suggests a different function from those unearthed in Cut 1. Pit D was located in square -B4 (first noted in the 25-50 cm. level), and measured 68x68 cm. in inner diameter and 80x88 cm. in outer diameter. The sides of the pit were lined down to the 70 cm. level with red clay mixed with stones. The lining measured 3 to 12 cm. in thickness, and the slightly insloping sides seem to have been relined several times. The base of the pit was not lined. Only one sherd was found in the pit itself. A small section of Pit E (ca. 10 cm.) was unearthed in square -B2, but most of it is in unexcavated square -A3. It was outlined by a circular area, roughly 55 cm. in diameter, of red clay beginning at the 45 cm. level. It seems to have been a feature similar to Pit D. Pit F was located in square -B2, just on the edge of square -B1, and seems to have been more like Pits A-C than Pits D and E. It was ca. 60x80 cm. in diameter and was at least 60 cm. deep. It was filled with dark earth mixed with chunks of red and yellow earth, and large and small white stones, and it stood out clearly from the surrounding soil. It contained much pottery, and probably was the source for a triple sided iron spear point and possibly two pieces of old glass.

The Layer A people also disturbed the earlier deposits when they set out storage jars. A large storage vessel, coated on the inside with bitumen, was found crushed in square -D3, and fragments of other storage vessels were also found.

Pits A-D and F seem to have been storage pits. Pits D and E could have been associated with the copper smelting that was going on at Zawi Chemi Shanidar at the time Layer A was being deposited (see Appendix II).

3.2. Layer B

Layer B, the Proto-Neolithic layer, started between 30 and 60 cm. below datum and continued down to sterile soil (figs. 4-6). Layer B was composed of very hard, brown colored, clayey earth. Soil change features within the layer were very difficult to distinguish because of the uniform toughness of the soil. The soil of Layer B was mixed with many rocks, reddened earth patches, charcoal bits, areas of crushed snail shell concentrations, much animal bones, and much cultural debris. Chipped, flaked and ground stone tools were found in good numbers. Bone tools were also characteristic, and there were a few made of antler and horn. There were some luxury items in the form of beads and pendants. The people of Layer B, on the basis of present knowledge, did not use ceramics, and in fact there was no associated clay objects of any sort (e.g. figurines, bracelets, etc.).

Crude stone architecture (Structure I) associated with Layer B, first noted in Test 1, was more fully outlined in the excavations of Cut 1 (pl. 3a,b, figs. 7-9). No architectural remains were uncovered in Cut 2. Structure I was rebuilt several times, with rough walls outlining a circular area roughly two meters in diameter. The walls were built of river boulders and other stones, apparently without the use of mortar. No definite fireplace or associated architectural features could be determined. Located just to the south of the earliest construction of Structure I was a mass of goat skulls and the wing bones from large predatory birds, suggesting some sort of special ritual (pl. 12).

Burned areas were found throughout Layer B. There was an extensive burned area to the east and southeast of the stone structure in Cut 1, as evidenced by the presence there of charcoal flecks, reddened earth, burned bones and fire cracked rocks. One hearth in this broad hearth area is centered in the northeast section of D1, continuing into C1 and E1, and also into -C1, -D1, and -E1, from the 75 to the 125 cm. level. A second hearth, or maybe an extension of the first, was located in the adjacent portion of D1 and E1, and into squares D2 and E2. This latter hearth area had large rocks mixed in it.

The earliest Zawi Chemi people dug broad shallow basins or pits into the almost sterile light-brown or red-brown soil found near the base of Cut 2 (pl. 1d, fig. 6). Three such basins were found in the northeastern part of Cut 2. In all cases they are filled with a dark colored earth, 15 to 35 cm. thick, which stands out clearly from the surrounding almost sterile, lighter colored soils. These basins were rich in animal bones and contained cultural remains; they extended to a depth of 1.90 m. below datum. Surrounding and below the basins were a series of variously colored soils. First there was a red-brown soil, then below a yellow-brown soil; sometimes these two graded into each other and were difficult to separate. These soils continued down to about the 2.50 m. level and contained scattered charcoal flecks, a few flints, and stray animal bones. Below was a light brown loamy soil, seemingly sterile.

CHAPTER 4

CULTURAL INVENTORY OF LAYER A

Layer A materials are found concentrated in the first fifty centimeters of the deposits, but stray pieces are found below because of such disturbances as pit digging and placement of large storage vessels. Pottery is the most numerous find, but iron, copper, and glass pieces are also present.

More than a dozen pieces of iron were recovered from the site. There are four spear points (pl. 2g,h). Two are large, flat, stemmed points (the complete one measures 11.9 cm. long with a stem 3.4 cm. long and 1.7 cm. wide). The other two are much smaller, three-sided points, triangular in section. One of them has a narrow groove in each side. There are several fragments which seem to be from such tools as nails, needles, screw drivers or pries. There is an iron ball, and a small piece of iron sheeting. There also is a piece of what looks like modern wire and a fragment of a metal band.

The copper or bronze objects found at the site are as follows: There are three copper coins, only one of which is well enough preserved to permit identification (pl. 2j and Appendix I). One coin was found in Pit B, one just below Pit C, and possibly the third one was also associated with the pits. There is an eyed needle, 7.4 cm. long (pl. 2i), and a piece of a bracelet.

Also associated with the Layer A deposits at the site are a number of pieces of slag, slag grading into baked clay lumps, and lumps of baked clay. Dr. Isabella Drew who analyzed these materials believes that they are evidence of copper smelting at Zawi Chemi Shanidar, during the Layer A occupation (see Appendix II).

There are about twenty tiny fragments of glass, most of which look like old glass pieces but a few are obviously modern. These are mainly from vessels, but there are bits of bracelets and one glass bead.

Other late period finds include: five pieces of rotary querns and what looks like a piece of knotted sinew. There are a number of fire flints and one possible gun flint.

The Layer A pottery includes a number of distinct types. The most diagnostic pottery is the so-called "Christian Ware," so named for the medallions with crosses or other designs impressed on it (pl. 2 c-f), for which a date of sixth to twelfth century has been suggested (Campbell Thompson and Mallowan, 1933). This ware has a widespread distribution in northern Iraq, and is apparently related to the series of old Christian settlements in the area. This type of decoration is usually found on fine ware vessels, but there is one example on a coarse ware vessel. The other fine wares may be plain or have simple fine-line combed decorations, or single incised curvilinear designs, or even punctate, gouged, or dashed designs. There is also some roulette decoration. There are a few glazed pieces, and some storage vessels were lined with a black substance (presumably bitumen).

Another characteristic pottery type is a medium to coarse grained plainware, heavily tempered with white grit. There are also large storage vessels, sometimes hand made, the surfaces coated the same black substance noted above. In one measurable example the mouth diameter is ca. 32.0 cm.

It is interesting to note that clay tobacco pipes are not found at Zawi Chemi Shanidar, so presumably the site was abandoned prior to the introduction of tobacco into the area. Fragments of such pipes have been recovered from the very top deposits at Shanidar Cave.

CHAPTER 5

CULTURAL INVENTORY OF LAYER B

Much cultural material was recovered from the Zawi Chemi occupation at the site. By far the majority of the tools were made out of stone, which for purposes of description in this report have been classified into the following lithic industries: chipped stone (sub-divided into microlithic and standard sized components); pecked, ground, or polished stone; and flaked stone. In the last named industry, medium to large sized flakes were removed from cores, and then either the flakes or the cores were utilized as tools. Bone, antler, horn, and ivory objects are present, and a small number of exotic or miscellaneous items are also associated with the Zawi Chemi culture.

5.1. Chipped Stone Industry[1]

Chipped stone tools are a basic part of the Zawi Chemi tool kit. They represent, however, a somewhat impoverished industry, in comparison to the preceeding Zarzi (Garrod, 1930), and for the most part are mediocre to poor in quality. There is much debitage and many cores, but purposely fashioned artifacts are not abundant. Both microlithic and standard sized components are present in the industry, but Zawi Chemi is not primarily a microlithic industry.

5.1.1. Microlithic Chipped Stone Industry[2]

The microlithic tools (Table 1) occur in a number of types, sub-types, and varieties, and are noteworthy for their small size. The term microlithic for this paper was arbitrarily applied to

---

[1] This study is based on a macroscopic analysis of the Zawi Chemi chipped stone tools, in accordance with the traditional morphological typology followed in Southwest Asian prehistory. It would be an interesting project to have microscopic use-wear/functional studies done on the tools and the debitage; this may be done in the future as part of a special project.

[2] It was not possible to screen all the dirt during the Spring 1957 season (Cut 1) because of the almost daily rains. This made the recovery of microlithic sized tools difficult during that season. All the dirt removed during the 1960 season (Cut 2) was screened and then checked through twice insuring the recovery of the microlithic industry. The counts given in the text and in table 1 refer only to Cut 2. Furthermore, Backed blades with snapped ends (IB) and Simple backed blades (IC) listed in table 1 with a single asterisk, were isolated in the U.S.A., and the counts given for them in table 1 refer only to that portion of the Cut 2 collection.

TABLE 1

Inventory of Microlithic Chipped Stone Tools – Cut 2

	Name	Numbers
I.	Backed blades	336
	A. retouched ends	80
	1. one retouched end	78
	a. regular	59
	b. gibbous	19
	2. two retouched ends	2
	B. snapped ends	51*
	C. simple backed blades	41*
	1. straight backed	18*
	2. convex backed	17*
	3. concave backed	3*
	4. gibbous	3*
II.	Backed flakes	3
III.	Lunates	111
IV.	Triangles	2
V.	Incomplete Triangle	1
VI.	Trapezoid	1
VII.	Borers	33
	A. double backed	27
	B. alternate backed	2
	C. alternate backed down one side	1
	D. notched	3
VIII.	Burins	3
IX.	Denticulates	28
X.	Notched pieces	11
XI.	Truncated pieces	17
	A. one truncated end	13
	B. two truncated ends	4
XII.	End scrapers	2
XIII.	Miscellany	2

*Counts refer only to Columbia University share of the Cut 2 collections.

blades measuring less than 3.0 cm. in length and to small sized flakes. The microlithic chipped stone tools may be described as follows:

I. *Backed blades* (fig. 10a-s) – This is the most numerous microlithic type and may be divided into three sub-types: retouched ends (IA); snapped ends (IB); and simple backed blades (IC).

IA. *retouched ends* (fig. 10a-i) – The blades in this, the most common sub-type, usually have one retouched end (IA1), but occasionally both ends are retouched (IA2). Most of the IA1 blades belong to the regular sub-variety (IA1a) and have one retouched end and a more-or-less straight backed side (fig. 10a-g). Rarely, both sides have been backed. Often the non-retouched end is narrowed to a point, sometimes accentuated by retouch along the non-backed side. The retouched end meets the backed side at an angle of 90° to 130°. The working side is thinner and shows little to heavy use wear. Some blades have retouch on this side near the ends, characteristically near the non-retouched end forming a pointed end as described above. The blades range in size from 1.0x0.4 cm. to 2.8x0.9 cm., with 1.6x0.4 cm. as an average. In the less common sub-variety with gibbosity (IA1b) the blades have a slight bump or swelling at the angle between the backed side and retouched end (fig. 10h,i). The angle at this point ranges from 100° to 155°. The backed side is characteristically concave, but in one case is slightly convex. The used side is thinner and shows use wear; and again retouch may be present towards the ends. The unretouched end is either pointed or broad. These blades range in size from 1.1x0.4 cm. to 2.0x0.4 cm., with 1.5x0.4 cm. as an average.

The backed blades with two retouched ends (IA2) occur only rarely. The two available specimens measure 1.9x1.0 cm. and 2.0x0.8 cm. The angles between the end and the backed side in one blade measure ca. 85° and ca. 115° in the other both are ca. 120°.

IB. *snapped ends* (fig. 10j-m) – The specimens classified here possibly are just broken backed blades. However, as they occur in quantity and are uniform in shape, I feel that they represent a distinct sub-type. They, in fact, resemble the backed blades with one retouched end (IA1), except that the broad end is not retouched but merely snapped. These blades have a more-or-less straight retouched back (a few are definitely concave), a narrowed pointed end, and a broad snapped end. The backed sides usually meet the snapped end at an angle of ca. 90°. The working edge has little to heavy use wear. Occasionally, there is some retouch on the used side near the narrowed end, making a sharp point at this end. These blades range in size from 0.9x0.4 cm. to 2.4x0.5 cm., with 1.6x0.4 cm. as an average.

IC. *simple backed blades* (fig. 10n-s) – Tools in this sub-type have been backed along one side but the ends have not been snapped or retouched. They occur in four varieties: straight backed (IC1); convex backed (IC2); concave backed (IC3); and gibbous (IC4). The blades in the IC1 variety (fig. 10n,o) usually have one backed side with one broad and one pointed end; rarely both ends are pointed. One specimen has steep retouch on both sides, possibly it was a micro-borer. The IC1 blades range in size from 1.3x0.4 cm. to 2.2x0.8 cm., with 1.8x0.5 cm. as an average. The IC2 blades (fig. 10p-r) are usually fully backed but may be only partly backed. They have convex or curved retouched backs, and either one pointed and one broad end, or two pointed ends. In the one double pointed specimen illustrated in figure 10r, there is some retouch on the unbacked side creating the distal pointed end. The IC2 blades range in size from 1.2x0.6 cm. to 2.7x0.9 cm., with 1.7x0.6 cm. as an average. The IC3 variety of backed blades is represented at most by only three specimens (two are broken so identification cannot be positive). The one complete blade measures 1.3x0.3 cm., but the two broken ones were wider. The IC4 variety (fig. 10s) is also represented by only three specimens. These blades have a bump or swelling in the middle of their backed side. The two measurable blades are 1.7x0.7 cm. and 1.0x0.8 cm.

II. *Backed flakes* – There are only three microlithic backed flakes, averaging 1.6x0.9 cm. in size. The working edge is considerably thinner than the backed side.

III. *Lunates* (fig. 10t-z) – These are a characteristic Zawi Chemi microlithic type. They have a fully retouched backed side, usually continuously rounded, but with occasional tendency to angularity. The used side is thinner, roughly straight (although actually it varies from slightly concave to slightly convex), and shows a little use wear. The lunates vary in size from 1.0x0.4 cm. to 1.7x0.5 cm., with 1.2x0.5 cm. as an average.

IV. *Triangles* (fig. 10aa,bb) – This is a rare microlithic type. The one complete triangle, measuring 1.6x0.7 cm., has two shorter concave backed sides and one longer, non-backed side; the latter is the working edge. The other triangle is broken but must have been slightly larger. It is similar in shape except that the retouched sides are straight rather than concave.

V. *Incomplete triangle* (fig. 10cc) – The one example is an incomplete triangle, in that in place of a third angle there is a broad end (the butt end of the flake). The two shorter sides of the piece are backed and the longer side is the working edge. This latter side is retouched for a short distance near the distal end, forming a point there. The specimen measures 2.2x1.3 cm.

VI. *Trapezoid* (fig. 10dd) – There is only one trapezoidal shaped microlith; it measures 2.3x1.0 cm. It resembles the triangles except that there is a fourth side, unretouched, between the two backed ones, parallel to the used side.

VII. *Borers* (fig. 10ee-kk) – This is a relatively common microlithic tool type, and may be divided into the following four sub-types:

VIIA. *double backed* (fig. 10ee,ff) – This is by far the most numerous microlithic borer sub-type. These borers are steeply retouched on both sides, characteristically down the full length or almost the full length. In a few, one side is more steeply retouched than the other. In shape they vary from parallel sided to an elongate triangle, expanding towards the butt end. In size they vary from 1.9x1.0 cm. to 2.7x0.5 cm., the former representing the ones with expanding butt ends.

VIIB. *alternate backed* (fig. 10gg,hh) – Two borers have been assigned to this sub-type, but one is a broken, worn specimen and its classification is not certain. They both have steep retouch along one side from the top surface, and flatter retouch along the opposite side from the bulbar surface. The complete specimen measures 2.3x0.6 cm., and is parallel sided with a retouched butt end.

VIIC. *alternate backed down one side* (fig. 10ii,jj) – The one example in the collection has steep retouch on most of one side on the obverse face, but down near the tip end of the side, 0.6 cm. from the tip, there is retouch on the bulbar face. The other side is completely retouched on the top surface. The piece measures 2.1x0.8 cm.

VIID. *notched borers* (fig. 10kk) – The borers in this sub-type have a steeply retouched notch on one side just below the point. The other side is not retouched. They seem to have been used as borers. They range in size from 2.0x0.7 cm. to 2.3x0.8 cm.

VIII. *Burins* (fig. 10ll) – These are small sized burins, not pieces made by the micro-burin technique. In at least two of them for sure, and perhps all three, the burin end seems to have been made by a lateral snap rather than a vertically directed burin blow. All have a backed side, and perhaps we are dealing here with backed pieces that have been broken in such a way that a burin end was accidently created. It should be noted, furthermore, that the tool illustrated in figure 10ll has a small retouched point opposite the burin end. These burins measure 1.4x0.8 cm., 1.9x0.9 cm., and 2.1x0.6 cm.

IX. *Denticulates* (fig. 10mm-pp) – These are more often on blades (21 examples) than on flakes (7 examples). The complete blades range in size from 2.4x1.2 cm. to 3.0x1.1 cm., and the flakes from 1.4x1.0 cm. to 2.4x1.3 cm. A few of the denticulations may have been due to use wear, but the majority of them seem to have been purposefully retouched.

X. *Notched pieces* (fig. 10qq) – Again these are more often on blades (7 examples) than on flakes (4 examples). The blades range in size from 2.0x0.9 cm. to 2.8x1.3 cm. In addition to a retouched notch some of these pieces also have use retouch.

XI. *Truncated pieces* (fig. 10rr,ss) – They may be divided into two sub-types: one truncated end (XIA) and two truncated ends (XIB). The former is more common, and is represented about equally by blades and flakes. The blades range in size from 2.0x0.8 cm. to 2.8x1.6 cm. Some of these pieces also show use wear. The XIB sub-type does not seem to have been as homogeneous as the XIA one. Two of the XIB specimens look like fragments of tools, truncated and reused. Another is a natually backed blade, truncated at both ends, with use retouch on the non-backed side. The fourth example is a thin but broad flake, both ends of which look truncated. Two of the pieces look rolled.

XII. *End scrapers* – Two specimens have been placed in this type, but one may be a broken piece from a regular sized end scraper. The complete one is a straight sided flake (1.6x1.0 cm.) with an end scraper at the distal end and with use retouch down the sides.

XIII. *Miscellany* – Here are placed two unique microlithic pieces not classifiable into one of the types described above.

In summary, a total of 550 microlithic sized chipped stone tools were found in Cut 2 at Zawi Chemi Shanidar. These occur in a number of types, which from archaeological evidence from other sites, we know were mounted in such cutting tools as knives and sickles or fitted into projectile heads. By far the greatest percentage of the Zawi Chemi microliths are backed blades of various kinds (61%); followed in popularity by the lunates (20%); various kinds of borers (6%); denticulates (5%); truncated pieces (3%); and backed flakes, triangles, incomplete triangles, trapezoids, burins, end scrapers, and miscellany in very small frequencies (each less than 1%).

5.1.2. Standard-sized Chipped Stone Industry

The standard-sized chipped stone industry of Zawi Chemi may be divided into thirteen types with a number of sub-types, as listed in Table 2[3]. The composite tools have been included with the type that seems to be the better represented on the tool, or the more numerous tool type. The denticulates and the related notched pieces are the most characteristic tools of the industry. The pièces esquillées are almost as numerous, but the function of these pieces pose an interesting problem which will be discussed later in the text. Scrapers of various types also occur in numbers at the site, and borers are well represented. The other tool types are relatively minor elements in the industry.

I. *Denticulates* (fig. 11) – This is the most characteristic Zawi Chemi tool type. Denticulates, as used in this paper, refer to those chipped stone specimens in which adjacent notches form points or teeth. There must be at least two such adjacent notches, but usually there is a whole series of them forming a toothed or denticulated edge. The notches usually vary in depth and width along the working edge, so that neat saw edges are not typical. The denticulated edges in most of these tools, I feel, were purposefully made, although some of the poorer examples may have been created through use. The denticulations are usually along the sides of these tools. Sometimes they are within a broad, shallow notch, usually at the distal end of a flake. Some of the denticulates also have regular use retouch, and in a small number a portion of the non-denticulated edge has been dulled through abrasion.

IA. *simple* (fig. 11a-l) – This is by far the most numerous denticulate sub-type. Simple denticulates occur on both blades and flakes, with the latter somewhat more common. The blades range in size from 3.8x1.3 cm. to 8.3x3.4 cm. The flakes are more variable in size and shape and seem to fall into two main groups. One is a thin to medium thick, medium-sized flake (ranging in size from 2.1x2.0 cm. to 5.2x3.1 cm.), with denticulations similar in size and shape to those found on the denticulate blades. Then there is a group of larger, thicker flakes, generally with coarser and rougher denticulations. These latter are often cortex flakes, and in a few cases seem to be close to the Steep scrapers. They range in size from 4.3x4.0 cm. to 6.9x3.0 cm.

IB. *alternate* (fig. 11m) – Usually occur on blades and may be divided into the following four varieties: alternate on both faces of the same side; alternate on opposite sides; alternate on both faces of one side and on both sides (fig. 11m); and alternate on both faces of both sides.

---

[3]The counts given in Table 2, unless otherwise noted, refer to the complete Cut 2 collection. For the descriptions of the tool types given below, however, all the excavated specimens were studied.

TABLE 2

Inventory of Standard-Sized Chipped Stone Tools – Cut 2

Name	Numbers
I. Denticulates	495
A. simple	413
B. alternate	9
C. on pièces esquillées	26*
D. with snapped ends	8**
E. and notched pieces	23
F. and notched and end scraper	1***
G. and side scrapers	10
H. and end scrapers	6
II. Notched pieces	61
A. simple	59
B. on a pièce esquillée	1
C. and side scraper	1
III. Side scrapers	145
A. simple	35****
B. heavy	27****
C. heavy and end scraper	1****
D. alternate	12****
E. bifacial	3****
F. bulbar	2****
G. thinned back	1****
H. on pièces espquillées	4****
I. on a truncated piece	1****
J. with snapped ends	13****
K. with snapped ends on a pièce esquilée	1****
IV. Steep scrapers	57
V. End scrapers	26
A. flake	20
B. blade	6
VI. Borers	45
A. double backed parallel sided	18
B. double backed triangular	9
C. double backed alternately backed on one side	6
D. alternate double backed	2
E. simple	4
VII. Burins	10
VIII. Backed blades	21
IX. Truncated backed blades	2
X. Truncated pieces	18

	Name	Numbers
XI.	Pièces esquillées	483
	A. with one edge battered	75****
	B. with two opposite edges battered	179****
	C. with two adjacent edges battered	2****
	D. with three edges battered	15****
	E. with four edges battered	8****
	F. core pieces	4****
XII.	Miscellany	50
XIII.	Broken tools	154

*Some of the specimens in the Iraq Museum collection may be snapped and, therefore, belong in sub-type ID.

**Four of these specimens are in the Columbia University collection and definitely belong here, the other four are in the Iraq Museum collection and were classified as Denticulated and truncated pieces, but may very well belong to this sub-type.

***Found only in Cut 1 (1956-1957 season) in the numbers given.

****Counts refer only to Columbia University half of the Cut 2 collection.

The one example of the last variety also has been truncated at the distal end. Also two of the tools in the third variety have been snapped at the distal end and the bulbar end has been thinned and part or all of the bulb has been removed.

IC. *on pièces esquillées* (fig. 11n-p) – Both flakes and chunks are present. The denticulate retouch is along one or both sides.

ID. *with snapped ends* (fig. 11q,r) – These are denticulated tools in which the ends have been snapped or retouched in some way. The snapped ends were then used as platforms from which broad, thinning flakes were struck, or for some purpose which produced battered retouch.

IE. *and notched* (fig. 11s) – Usually occur on blades but are also found on flakes. Tools with a notch on one side and a denticulated area on the other side seem most numerous. Other varieties include: notch and denticulate on the same side; and notch at the end of the flake and denticulations along the sides.

IF. *notched and end scraper* (fig. 11t) – The one example is a blade, measuring 5.1x2.0 cm. One side has a broad, shallow retouched notch and a series of denticulations. The distal end, although partly broken, seems to have been an end scraper.

IG. *and side scraper* (fig. 11u) – These seem to occur mainly on blades, but are also found on flakes. Characteristic are those that are denticulated on one side and a scraper on the other side. Other combinations such as the following are also present: one side is a scraper while the other is a denticulate and a scraper; one side is a denticulate while the other is a denticulate and a scraper; and the denticulate and scraper are both on the same side.

Both regular and heavy scraper retouch occur. Several of the tools, however, have weak retouch and are poor examples.

IH. *and end scrapers* (fig. 11v) – Characteristically occur on blades. One or both sides are denticulated and the ends are concave, convex, or oblique scrapers. The two concave specimens have a little point or hook at one end of the end scraper, which is worthy of special note (fig. 11v).

II. *Notched pieces* (fig. 12a-f) – Although related to the denticulates and sometimes used in combination with them, the notched tools seem to be distinctive. They are a rare type, occurring with only about one/eighth the frequency. They generally are crude tools, and in some cases the notches could have been made accidentally or through use. They have one or more retouched notches, varying from small deep notches to broad, shallow ones. The three sub-types may be briefly described as follows:

IIA. *simple* (fig. 12a-e) – This is by far the most numerous sub-type. Both flakes and blades are used, but the former are almost twice as common. Usually there is only one notch per specimen, characteristically on the side but occasionally at the end. A few tools have one notch on either side, these could be more-or-less opposite each other but they do not have to be, and one specimen has two notches on the same side. Usually the notches are on the obverse face, but may occur on the bulbar face. The flakes range from 2.7x1.7 cm. to 6.2x3.6 cm. The one complete blade measures 3.2x1.5 cm., but there are broken sections of larger blades.

IIB. *on a pièce esquillée* (fig. 12f) – The one specimen has a single notch on the side and battering at the ends; it measures 2.8x1.7 cm.

IIC. *and side scraper* – The one such tool available for study is a large, broken specimen and has a notch and a side scraper on the same side.

III. *Side scrapers* (figs. 12g-r and 13a-f) – This is another common Zawi Chemi tool type. Eleven side scraper sub-types may be described for the Zawi Chemi collection.

IIIA. *simple* (fig. 12g,h) – This is the most numerous side scraper sub-type. Both single and double scrapers are present, but the former are almost twice as common. Simple side scrapers usually occur on blades but some flakes are present. The tools tend to have weak to moderate scraper retouch, which distinguishes them from the heavy side scrapers described immediately below. The complete blades range in size from 4.1x1.6 cm. to 8.7x2.3 cm. and the flakes from 2.8x1.8 cm. to 4.2x3.1 cm. In addition to the scraper edges many of these tools show use retouch.

IIIB. *heavy* (fig. 12i-l) – This is the second most common side scraper sub-type. Single and double examples occur with about equal frequency. The characteristic feature about these tools is that they have heavy, high, and often step-like retouch. Usually they are on large and/or thick flakes and blades, with the blades somewhat more common than the flakes. The two measurable flakes are 5.3x2.8 cm. and 6.2x5.7 cm., and the one measurable blade is 9.0x3.3 cm. The single scrapers may be concave, convex, or straight; and the double scrapers may be double concave (almost strangled) or concavo-convex. Concave scrapers seem to have been favored.

IIIC. *heavy and end scraper* (fig. 12m) – In the one example, one side is a heavy concave scraper and the other is a heavy convex scraper, and the broad distal end is a steep end scraper. The tool measures 7.3x3.4 cm.

IIID. *alternate* (fig. 12n-p) – These occur on blades (most common), flakes, and occasionally on pièces esquillées. The blades range from 4.6x1.9 cm. to large ones more than 7.8 cm. long; and the two flakes which could be measured are 1.3x2.4 cm. and 1.9x3.6cm. Characteristically, opposite sides are retouched, but sometimes the same side can be alternately retouched. Some of the fragmentary specimens on thick, narrow pieces (fig. 12n,o) may have been from thick, piercing tools rather than side scrapers.

IIIE. *bifacial* (fig. 12q) – All three examples available for study were found in the 75-100 cm. level of Cut 2. Two of them are very similar. They have a heavy scraper along one side and a simple scraper along the other side; the latter side also has, on the bulbar surface, retouch thinning the edge and giving it a sinuous contour. This edge also shows evidence of abrasion. Both tools are snapped across one end, but I could not determine if this was purposeful or accidental. The two tools measure 4.0x2.3 cm. and 3.0x1.7 cm. The third example is similar to the two already described, but is not as good a specimen.

IIIF. *bulbar* – Two are poorly made flake tools (averaging 3.8x2.4 cm.) possibly just used pieces, one side of which shows retouch from the bulbar face. The one blade specimen 5.7x1.5 cm.) has neat scraper retouch on the bulbar face along one side and continuing around the pointed bulbar end. The other side has ca. 1.5 cm. of retouch on the obverse face down from the pointed end; the rest of this side is naturally backed.

IIIG. *thinned back* – The one example available for study is made on a naturally backed blade; the backed side has been thinned by flat retouch from the bulbar surface.

IIIH. *on pièces esquillées* – Only one of the specimens available for study is complete; it is a double side scraper (concavo-convex) on a pièce esquillée.

IIII. *on a truncated piece* (fig. 12r) – There is only one example available for study; it is a flat, double sided scraper with one truncated end.

IIIJ. *with snapped ends* (fig. 13a-f) – The Zawi Chemi knappers sometimes snapped the ends of their tools, making roughly rectangular or even squarish shaped pieces with straight ends. Often the snapped ends exhibit a hinged fracture. The snapped ends could then be modified by retouch, varying from weak, small flake removal to heavy battering. In order to distinguish these scrapers from those made on pièces esquillées I have used the following rule. If the scalar retouch occurs on a snapped end it was placed in this sub-type, but if the scalar retouch is on an unsnapped end it was placed in Side scraper sub-type IIIH.

Four varieties of scrapers with snapped ends may be outlined. In the first variety (fig. 13a, b) both ends are snapped and battered. The two illustrated specimens are so similar that they look like they were made by the same hand. They are heavy side scrapers (one is single and the other double), measuring 4.5x2.7 cm. and 4.0x3.0 cm. Both have one thick snapped and retouched end with a hinge fracture and one thinned, snapped end with heavy pièce esquillée retouch. In the second variety (fig. 13c,d) both ends are snapped but only one is battered. Characteristically, they are square to rectangular shaped scrapers (ranging from 2.5x2.7 cm. to 4.8x2.6 cm.) and flattish in section. The retouch on the battered end varies from pièce esquillée-like retouch on both faces to weak, flat thinning only on the bulbar face. One example is an alternate side scraper. In the third variety only one end is snapped and battered, with weak battering from the top surface. One example also has been considerably thinned on the bulbar face, at the unsnapped end. In the fourth variety (fig. 13e) there are two snapped, retouched ends and in addition some side thinning. Usually they seem to be smallish to medium sized, flat tools with bulbar side thinning. There is also a large, heavy piece with obliquely snapped ends which give it a trapezoidal shape (fig. 13f). The longer side is a heavy side scraper and the shorter side has been thinned from both faces.

IIIK. *with snapped ends on a pièce esquillée* – There is only one such piece available for study. It is a single scraper with one snapped end and one pièce esquillée end.

IV. *Steep scrapers* (fig. 13g-k) – Although this is a somewhat heterogeneous type, all the tools placed here have both high core-like retouch and also low, abrupt retouch just along the working edge. It is because of the presence of the latter feature that they have been classified as scrapers rather than cores. Some in fact may have been cores reused as scrapers or just cores. Sometimes such tools have been called "core scrapers" in the literature. Most are crude specimens but a few are well made.

Steep scrapers occur on thick flakes, many are core flakes or core pieces, or even cores. They range in size from 1.9x2.2 cm. to 3.1x3.6 cm. and in greatest thickness from 1.2 to 3.1 cm. They are characteristically highly plano-convex in section. Usually the distal end and part of the sides are used. Although the obverse face is high to accomodate the steep retouch, it often is modified apparently to make the tool more handy to use. It could be partly or completely flat across the top, made so by purposeful retouch, or by the choice of a suitable shaped stone. In some specimens, however, it could rise to a central apex, making the piece cone shaped. In the flat topped examples the thickest point is near the scraper end, while in the conical ones it is in the center. The bulbar face may be but usually is not retouched, but in one example the scraper is on the bulbar surface (fig. 13j).

A few of these tools are retouched primarily along the sides, with the ends little or not used at all. Perhaps they should form a separate sub-type. A few are so markedly denticulate (fig. 13k) that perhaps they too form a sub-type.

V. *End scrapers* (fig. 13l,m) – They are divided into two sub-types on the basis of blank shape.

VA. *flake* (fig. 13l) – These are poorish quality tools, with weak scraper retouch at one end; one seems to be nosed (fig. 13l). They vary in size from 2.4x2.2 cm. to 5.1x3.4 cm.

VB. *blade* (fig. 13m) – These are also poorish quality tools, with weak retouch. One seems to have been snapped off at the bulbar end (fig. 13m). The two complete blade end scrapers measure 3.1x1.5 cm., but one of the broken ones is more than 5.7 cm. long.

VI. *Borers* (fig. 13n-t) – These are one of the better made Zawi Chemi chipped stone tool types. Five borer sub-types have been identified in the Zawi Chemi tool kit.

VIA. *double backed parallel sided* (fig. 13n) – This, the most common borer sub-type, is characterized by narrow, elongated, more-or-less parallel sided, completely backed tools. The unbroken borers range in size from 2.9x0.8 cm. to 5.7x1.2 cm., but some of the broken ones were from even larger, broader tools. These latter are possibly related to the so-called "fabricators" of the Natufian (Garrod and Bate, 1937, p. 35).

VIB. *double backed triangular* (fig. 13o,p) – These are similar to the borers in sub-type VIA, but are shorter (average 3.0x1.4 cm.) and have a roughly triangular shape with a broad butt end. Their sides may be completely or only partly backed. One borer has a definite notch just below the point (fig. 13p), and a few specimens are concave along one side, suggesting broad, shallow notches.

VIC. *double backed, alternately backed on one side* (fig. 13q,r) – These borers are alternaely backed on one side and normally backed on the other side. The point is characteristically formed by retouch from both faces, therefore, it also is alternately retouched.

VID. *double backed borers, alternately backed on both sides* – Both examples in this sub-type are broken, but enough is present to determine that both sides are alternately retouched. The tip itself is formed by retouch from only the top surface, so it is not alternately retouched.

VIE. *simple borers* (fig. 13s,t) – This is a heterogeneous group into which all the non-backed borers have been placed. In one variety the end of a flake is retouched or notched in such a way as to form a rough point (fig. 13s). Then there are two roughly elongated, triangular shaped flakes that seem to have been used as borers or reamers with little or no retouch (fig. 13t). Interestingly enough, both pieces were struck from the same core. There is also a naturally backed, irregular shaped blade with some weak alternate retouch and a narrowed point which seems to have been used as a borer.

VII. *Burins* (fig. 14a-c) – A small number of poorly made burins are present in the Zawi Chemi collections. Two are angle burins on a snapped end (fig. 14a,b). In one (fig. 14a) the end opposite the burin end is a pièce esquillée. There are two angle burins on a retouched truncation, one concave and one convex. There is also one possible angle burin made on a thin blade, snapped at both ends. The burin end has a straight retouched truncation, from which two burin-like blows have been struck; and the opposite end has been snapped with a hinge fracture and has pièce esquillée-like retouch. There are three dihedral burins and two very similar polyhedral carinate burins on core pieces (fig. 14c). There is one combination Noailles burin and notched blade and also one fragmentary specimen that looks like a combin-ation burin and notched blade. There are also a small number of burin spalls in the collection.

VIII. *Backed blades* (fig. 14d) – Perhaps these tools should be divided into two sub-types; those with more-or-less straight backs (the more common sub-type) and those with curved backs (resembling lunates). The one complete, straight backed blade measures 3.0x1.0 cm. These backed blades range in width from 0.7 to 1.6 cm., noticeably larger than the microlithic ones. The one complete curved backed blade measures 3.1x1.2 cm., and has retouch from both faces; the other one is a fragmentary example of a crude specimen. The tool illustrated in figure 14d probably also belongs here. This crescent-shaped piece, measureing 3.4x4.1 cm. was made by removing the butt end of a small flake and retouching that end to form a broad, curved side. The straight (or distal end) of the piece is also retouched. All sides of the piece, in fact, show steep retouch or backing, so perhaps the two pointed ends (both broken) were the working parts of the tool.

IX. *Truncated backed blades* (fig. 14e) – This is a rare type. The one complete example measures 3.2x1.1 cm., and has a straight truncated retouched end. The second specimen (fig. 14e) is broken, but the one remaining end is truncated obliquely.

X. *Truncated pieces* – These are not very distinctive tools, but all have one end partly or wholly truncated. The truncations could be oblique, concave, or straight. Flakes are more common than blades; the former range from 2.0x1.6 cm. to 2.9x2.2 cm., and the latter from 3.5x1.4 cm. to 4.3x1.4 cm.

XI. *Pièces esquillées* (fig. 14f-q) – This is the second most common chipped stone type at Zawi Chemi; only the denticulates occur in more numbers. Usually these pieces are made on roughly rectangular or even square flakes, but core pieces or even cores are present. The pièces esquillées (also called scalar pieces) are crude specimens with characteristic battered or stepped edges. The battering may be bifacial or unifacial, with the latter by far more common. A thinned edge is achieved by this battering, but it is not known if this edge was created purposefully or was accidentally achieved as the piece was being used. A few show ordinary use retouch in addition to the characteristic battering, and a small number were used as denticulates, side scrapers, etc.

The pieces classified in this tool type are, therefore, varied, and it seems likely that not all were made in the same way or used for the same purpose. Perhaps they should not be lumped together as they are here and have been in other studies. However, until more work is done on these pieces with their distinctive battered retouch, it still seems useful to describe them together as a unit.

Pièces esquillées have been identified as belonging to a distinct type since they were first described by Bardon and Bouyssonie (1906). They occur in many parts of the Old World in both palaeolithic and epi-palaeolithic contexts. A number of different usages for these tools have been suggested; the more common ones being that they were used as the intermediate member in the indirect percussion flaking process or that they were used as some sort of a chisel. J.P. White (1968) on the basis of field observations of flint knapping among the Duna people living today in the Western Highlands of New Guinea, suggests that the scalar pieces are debris fragments resulting from the bi-polar flaking technique. The scalar pieces are part of the flaking debris not utilized by the Duna people at all; in fact they are only interested in the flakes removed from the core in the knapping process. White does not suggest that all scalar pieces are "waste-product cores," carefully limiting himself to such objects from the New Guinea and Australian regions. This interpretation may be valid for some of the scalar pieces on cores, but cannot be true for most of them, especially the thin flakes. Although certainly some sort of sharp blow was necessary to achieve the characteristic battered look of these pieces, we still do not know precisely how these pieces were made or how they were used. Tixier (1963, pp. 146-149) rejects the probability of a relationship between the scalar pieces and the bi-polar flaking technique. He believes that the use of these tools is still not fully understood, suggesting that perhaps they were used in the manufacture of some perishable materials. Interestingly enough, Tixier (Ibid.) also points out that these scalar pieces are characteristic of the Ibero Maurusian industries of North Africa, roughly contemporary with Zawi Chemi.

The Zawi Chemi pièces esquillées may be divided into six sub-types:

XIA. *one edge battered* (fig. 14f) – Many of the tools placed here are broken and, therefore, may belong to one of the other sub-types. Most are thin flakes, but some are thick flakes, and a few are core rejuvenation pieces or even cores. They range in size from 1.6x1.6 cm. to 4.3x5.0 cm. A small number of them have use retouch along the unbattered sides.

XIB. *two opposite edges battered* (fig. 14g-m) – This is by far the most common sub-type. Flat, rectangular flakes are characteristic, although there are some thicker ones. A few of these latter seem to be on core pieces, with the scalar retouch on a flat edge (in three cases on the striking platform). The tools in this sub-type range in size from 1.5x1.4 cm. to 3.4x4.1 cm., but broken specimens suggest that larger ones were known. Use retouch occurs occasionally on these tools. Two of them are unusual in that they have heavy use or scraper retouch along one side; also these same retouched sides have been dulled through some sort of abrasion (fig. 14m).

XIC. *two adjacent edges battered* (fig. 14n) – The two such specimens available for study are chunky flakes, possibly broken, measuring 4.0x2.7 cm. and 4.0x4.9 cm.

XID. *three edges battered* (fig. 14o-q) – These are all flakes, characteristically roughly rectangular in shape. They range in size from 1.9x2.1 cm. to 5.3x3.6 cm. Some of the broken ones possibly belong to sub-type XIE.

XIE. *four edges battered* – These are obviously re-used cores.

XII. *Miscellany* – This is a catch-all group, not an artifact type. Here are placed such miscellany as the follows:

Pieces with worn edges – Some part of the edge has been dulled through abrasion or wear of some sort. A few have use wear, and occasionally the abrasion has even dulled the working edge.

Pieces with sickle sheen – There are two small fragments with weak sickle sheen along the sides.

Raclettes – Two possible broken raclettes are present.

Pointed flakes – These are flakes with weak retouch along the sides to form a point at the end. One has alternate retouch, and one a weak facetted butt.

Pieces with heavy retouch – These are small fragments from well made tools with heavy, steep retouch along both sides. They may be from heavy side scrapers or even notch and/or denticulate tools, but the tapering end of one of them suggests that specimen at least may be a a piece of a heavy piercing tool (fabricator).

Unique tools – One is a broad flake, 4.3x3.8 cm., retouched on the distal end, from the bulbar surface in two places, and then from the top surface in the area in between the two bulbar retouched spots, giving a sinuous edge. There is also a core rejuvenation piece with heavy battering from both faces, showing that the piece was used after removal from the core. The rest of the pieces placed here are miscellaneous worked specimens.

XIII. *Broken tools* – Here are placed all the bits of broken tools, too fragmentary to classify. They seem for the most part, to be from denticulates, notched pieces, or side scrapers.

The standardized-sized Zawi Chemi chipped stone industry may be summarized briefly as follows. The total of 1567 such tools found in Cut 2 were divided into eleven distinctive tool types (about half divisible into sub-types); a miscellaneous category including odd specimens; and a fairly large number of tool fragments which could not be classified because of their fragmentary condition. The denticulates(31.6%) and the related notched tools (3.9%) form the largest category of tools (35.5%) in the Zawi Chemi tool kit. Also common are the pièces esquillées (30.8%), but as already discussed, this is not a homogeneous type and also one with interpretative problems. Although some of the Zawi Chemi pièces esquillées may have been the result of the knapping process, others were certainly purposely fashioned for some use.

Scrapers are also a characteristic Zawi Chemi tool type (14.4%), with side scrapers (9.2%) the most common type (divided into a number of specialized sub-types). Steep scrapers (3.6%) although heterogeneous in form also seem important in the Zawi Chemi tool kit. Although small numbers of end scrapers (1.6%) are present at Zawi Chemi Shanidar, they are characteristically rough, poorly made tools, with weak retouch. Perhaps the steep scrapers performed some of the functions, in earlier periods, done by the end scrapers.

Borers are a small but characteristic Zawi Chemi tool type (3.0%), and represent some of the best made of the chipped stone tools found at the site. The small number of burins present (0.6%) are poorish in quality. Backed blades (1.3%), truncated backed blades (0.1%), and truncated pieces (1.1%) all occur in only relatively small amounts.

The miscellaneous type (3.2%) includes a number of odd pieces, the most interesting of which may be summarized here. Pieces with dulled edges, even sometimes on an old sharp working edge, suggest hafted pieces or reworked pieces. Interestingly enough, only two small fragments with weak sickle sheen are present, so the question of a Zawi Chemi reaping tool is still an open one. Also of interest are the pieces with heavy steep retouch, some of which may be from fabricators.

5.1.3. Cores

Cores (pl. 13) are well represented at Zawi Chemi Shanidar, indicating that knapping was done at that site. The large amount of chipping debitage, of course, reinforces this conclusion. It seems that most of the cores are made from river pebbles, and for that reason exhibit a great deal of variety in color and texture. Some special material may have been traded in–e.g., the good quality, fine grained, gray chert from which many of the larger tools are made. The Zawi Chemi people must have tried to extract as many usable pieces from their cores as possible, since most are worked down to small size and some to nubbins. None of the hundreds of cores recovered at the site was big enough to produce the good sized blades used for some of the tools.

Those core-like specimens with obvious scraper retouch have already been described as steep scrapers (fig. 13g-k), type IV in Table 2, but some of those included here as cores may, in fact, also have been used as scrapers. The Zawi Chemi cores may be divided into the types listed in Table 3.

I. *Single platform–incompletely retouched* (pl. 13a-e) – This is the most common core type. Characteristically a pebble is split, or a flake or flakes are removed from one of the ends of a pebble to form the core. A few such cores are made on thick flakes or chunks. Blades and flakes are removed from around part of the perimeter of the striking platform, but there is always some cortex area not utilized. Because of the small size of these cores, in height (from striking platform to apex) they range from 1.5 to 4.6 cm., with 2.8 cm. as an average, most of these cores must have been used, in their present states, for the extraction of microlithic sized blades and flakes. They may have plain (pl. 13a,b,e) or prepared (pl. 13c,d) striking platforms, with the former somewhat more common. The plain platforms are most often slightly concave, but flat ones are almost as common, and convex ones the least common. The flake cores all have convex striking platforms. In the cores with prepared platforms, long, shallow flakes are removed from the platform until the desired shaping or reshaping is achieved. Characteristically only part of the platform is prepared.

II. *Single platform–completely retouched* (pl. 13f,g) – Such cores are much less common than those with incompletely retouched platforms. Most are made on split pebbles, but a few may be on chunks or thick flakes. These cores are used for flake or blade removal completely around the perimeter of the platform. They tend to be pyramidal in shape, and may have some cortex remaining at the apex. Again the size of these cores, 1.7 to 3.5 cm. in height, with 2.4 cm. as an average, tends to pretty much limit them to microlithic production. These cores may have either plain (pl. 13f) or prepared (pl. 13g) platforms, with the latter more common. The unprepared cores are used just as they are split. Most of them have concave platforms, but a few flat or even convex ones are present.

III. *Two platform* (pl. 13h-j) – This is another common core type at Zawi Chemi Shanidar, and may be divided into the following three sub types: A. platforms meet at a right angle; B. platforms meet at an angle greater than 90°; and C. platforms meet at an angle less than 90°.

IIIA. *platforms meet at a right angle* (pl. 13h) – This is by far the most common of the two platform core sub-types. The two platforms meet at a right angle, more-or-less. Most seem to be

TABLE 3

Inventory of Cores[1]

	Names	Numbers
I.	Single Platform–Incompletely Retouched	128
II.	Single Platform–Completely Retouched	35
III.	Two Platform	104
IV.	Three Platform	53
V.	Four Platform	10
VI.	Miscellaneous	11

[1]The classification of the cores given here is based on the entire Zawi Chemi collection but the counts refer to only that half of the Cut 2 collection presently at Columbia University. In addition to the numbers counted above, there are also 88 broken cores or core pieces and 13 pebbles which have been split but not used as core:, in that collection.

single platform cores to which a second platform is added. Sometimes part of the original platform is removed and a second platform created at right angles to it. In another variety, the shape of the core itself is appropriate for the utilization of a second platform, at right angles to the first; in such cases part of the area used for flake and blade removal is turned into the second platform.

IIIB. *platforms meet at an angle greater than 90°* (pl. 13i) – These cores are prepared in such a way that the two platforms meet at an angle greater than 90° (range is from 105° to 135°. This is the least common of the two platform core sub-types.

IIIC. *platforms meet at an angle less than 90°* (pl. 13j) – In these cores the two platforms meet, or would meet if extended, at angle less than 90°. The working part of the two striking platforms are, in fact, characteristically roughly opposite each other, so in a sense, they can be thought of as bipolar cores.

IV. *Three platform* (pl. 13k) – This is a relatively common Zawi Chemi type. The cores are variable in shape and size.

V. *Four platform* (pl. 13l) – This is a rare Zawi Chemi core type; the examples are variable in shape and size.

VI. *Miscellaneous* (pl. 13m) – Here we have a number of minor types represented by a few specimens each. There are amorphous chunk cores, i.e., those chunks with flakes removed in no apparent pattern or in the process of being reshaped. There are also a couple cores I call discoid-bipolar (pl. 13m). These are roughly disc-shaped cores with flake removal from two opposite ends on one face. One has a plain and one a prepared striking platform. Then there are six nubbin cores, too small to classify.

5.1.4. Use Retouched Pieces

Many, chipped pieces were used without special shaping. They could show little to heavy evidence of use retouch, and vary from pieces lightly used to long, regular, naturally backed blades with heavy use retouch. The following counts represent the pieces with use retouch from Cut 2: There is a total of 3,894 pieces that show use retouch broken down into the following blank shapes: 535 blades; 1,503 flakes; 1,217 broken pieces from either flakes or blades; 350 microlithic blades; 225 microlithic flakes; 2 broken pieces from either microlithic flakes or blades; and 62 core rejuvenation pieces or other core pieces.

5.1.5. Debitage

Chipping debris is abundant at Zawi Chemi Shanidar, suggesting that knapping was done at the site. Somewhat over 18,000 pieces of knapping debris are present in the Columbia University half of the Cut 2 collections; i.e., from an area four meters by eight meters, excavated in part to a depth of 2.50 m. Some 95% of this debris was found in the .50–1.50 m. level at the site; i.e., the main part of the Zawi Chemi occupation (Layer B). The small numbers found in Layer A were either intrusive from Layer B or could be a product of more recent knapping (e.g. fire flints or gun flints). The chipping debris from the lower levels at the site are associated with the pits dug into native soil by the Zawi Chemi people.

5.1.6. Summary of the Zawi Chemi Chipped Stone Industry

Although the Zawi Chemi chipped stone industry appears to be related to the earlier Zarzi industry, except for some small numbers of well made tools, it gives the impression of being an impoverished industry and does not exhibit the same knapping proficiency or evident interest in chipped stone tools characteristic of the earlier Zarzi. The Zawi Chemi industry, however, still contains both a microlithic and a standard-sized component. As we shall see below, new stone working techniques were introduced at this time and there was much experimentation in making tools with these new lithic techniques.

The most common chipped stone tools at Zawi Chemi Shanidar, the denticulates and the notched pieces, are thought to be wood-working tools, as probably also are some of the borers. Evidence suggests that the area was wooded during the time of the Zawi Chemi occupation. The axes, addzes, and related tools discussed in the next section of this report lend additional support to a heavy wood-working industry at Zawi Chemi Shanidar. The various kinds of scrapers and also the borers suggest a skin working industry, and we know from the abundant faunal remains found at the site that animal skins were certainly available to the Zawi Chemi people. No definite projectile points (either for arrows or spears) were found, although there are two flakes, weakly retouched to form a point at one end. Also of interest is the lack of blades with sickle sheen, except for two fragmentary specimens exhibiting weak sheen. This puzzle is compounded by the discovery of a bone haft at the site (pl. 11b,c) which could have been used as a sickle. We know that the Zawi Chemi people were reaping plant food of some kind, for we have the mullers (pl. 4a-d) and querns (pl. 4e-i) that they used for the preparation of such foods.

Much flint debris was found at the site, indicating that the knapping was done there. We also know that they utilized large numbers of unshaped flakes and blades for a variety of jobs, for many of these specimens with evidence of use wear also have been recovered.

5.2. Pecked, Ground, or Polished Stone Industry

Many tools fashioned by these techniques were found at Zawi Chemi Shanidar, and many man hours of labor must have gone into their manufacture. Such tools must have been important to the Zawi Chemi people. It is important, furthermore, to note that this is the first time that tools made by these techniques are characteristic of human cultures. They represent a whole new inventory of tools, indicating not only new lithic techniques but a new way of life.

Eighteen distinctive types have been described for these stone tools (see Table 4), reflecting varied tools with widely differing functions. They range from small, decorative objects such as beads or pendants; to food preparation tools such as querns and mullers; to a variety of pecking, pounding, and hammering tools; as well as to a number of types of uncertain functions.

I. *Mullers* (pl. 4a-d) – Mullers or hand grinding stones are found in great numbers at Zawi Chemi Shanidar (more than 250 of them have been recorded from the excavations), indicating that they played an important economic role in the life of the village. The large numbers recovered also suggest that the site may have been a manufacturing center for mullers. The mullers are made of quartzite, and many man hours must have gone into their manufacture. The fact that there are at least four sub-types of mullers, further divisible into varieties, suggests specialization for food type or process. Gould, Koster, and Sontz reporting on the use of hand grinders among the modern Australian aborigines note that (Gould, Koster, and Sontz, 1971, p. 164):

> "Different seeds and nuts require different motions of grinding. For instance, the preparation of seed-paste from sun-dried *kampurarpa* (Solanum sp.) fruit involved a motion in which the grinder, held by both hands, is pushed and rotated vertically in an arc of about 30° from back to front at the same time. Continued use of this kind gives the pebble a smooth, convex surface. On the other hand, the grinding of *kalpari* (Chenopodium rhadinostachyum) and some other seeds is performed with a simple back-and-forth motion on a flat plane, causing a fairly flat surface to form on the pebble."

They (Gould, Koster, and Sontz, 1971, p. 164) also note that some of the grinders have small depressions on the center of their flat face where nuts have been pounded. This reminds one of the Zawi Chemi pitted mullers described below (pl. 4c,d). Occasionally the Zawi Chemi mullers were used also as hammerstones.

The Zawi Chemi mullers may be divided into the following four sub-types: A. double faced, B. single faced, C. double pitted, and D. single pitted.

IA. *double faced* (pl. 4a) – These are pecked on both faces and around the sides, and seemingly were used on both faces. They range in size from 9.9x10.6x5.3 cm. to 11.1x11.2x5.4 cm. They may be bi-flat, plano-convex, bi-convex, or concavo-convex in section, and circular or ovate in shape. Some have a polish or sheen on their surfaces from use.

IB. *single faced* (pl. 4b) – These have only one pecked working face; the other is either completely unmodified or may have some pecking around the periphery but with a large unmodified central portion. The sides are usually pecked. The mullers range in size from 8.7x10.4x5.6 cm. to 12.1x12.6x6.0 cm. They may be plano-convex, bi-flat, or bi-convex in section, and either circular or ovate in shape. Two of the bi-convex mullers are worthy of special note. They lack the usual vertical sides of the other mullers, instead the upper and lower faces meet each other. Both specimens are broken off at one end, but it could not be determined if this was accidental or purposeful.

IC. *double pitted* (p. 4c) – These mullers have a single pit on both faces, which may vary from a mere shallow roughening to a distinct pit as much as 0.5 cm. deep. The pitted surface may be otherwise unmodified or may have slight or all-over pecking. Some surfaces have a sheen or lustre from use. The sides have been partly or completely pecked. These mullers range in size from 7.0x8.4x4.5 cm. to 10.3x11.7x5.9 cm.

ID. *single pitted* (pl. 4d) – These mullers have single pits on one face only. The pit may vary from a mere shallow roughening to a distinct, shaped pit as much as 0.4 cm. deep. The pitted surface could be pecked or otherwise unmodified. Usually the sides have been pecked all around. The muller face is pecked, and is characteristically flat but may be convex. These mullers are either ovate or circular in shape, and some have a polish or sheen. An interesting specimen from Cut I shows heavy battering at one end, and also has two opposed battered areas on the sides, giving the appearance of notches. The single pitted mullers range in size from 8.6x9.6x5.2 cm. to 10.2x10.7x5.1 cm.

II. *Querns* (pl. 4e-i) – Seventeen querns are represented in the Cut 2 collections; thirteen from Cut 1; and more than sixty quern fragments were picked up from the surface of the site. Again the large numbers of such tools suggest they played an important role in the economy of the people, and also that this may have been a manufacturing center for querns. The size and weight of the querns, further, indicates that the Zawi Chemi people were at least a semi-sedentary people.

The Zawi Chemi querns are characteristically made from quartzite boulders, roughly ovate or rectangular shaped, and probably also circular. They were pecked to the desired shape for grinding use. Sometimes the base was flattened as a convenience. Occasionally, the sides are flaked, with spalls removed, but it is not known if this was done while the piece was functioning as a quern or subsequently.

Modern rotary type querns made of a local conglomerate are found in Layer A and on the surface of the site.

TABLE 4

Inventory of Pecked, Ground, or Polished Stone Tools[1]

Name	Numbers
I. Mullers	64[2]
A. double faced	21
B. single faced	13
C. double pitted	6
D. single pitted	10
II. Querns	13
A. trough	8
B. flat	1
C. bifacial	1*
D. combination quern-mortar	4
III. Mortar	1
IV. Bowl	1
V. Abraders	22
A. pebble	7
B. large pebble	2
C. partly pecked	7
D. pecked	5
E. combination pebble abraber-pecking stone	1
VI. Pounders	6
VII. Hammerstones	41
A. simple	10
B. single pitted	2
C. double pitted	2
D. greenstone	27
VIII. Pecking Stones	22
A. simple	10
B. elongate pebble	4
C. pecking stone–choppers	5
D. pecking stone–rubbers	3
E. pecking stone–facetted rubber	1**
F. notched	2***
IX. Rubbers	26
A. facetted	22
B. simple	4
X. Rings	4****
XI. Cupped Stones	3****
XII. Shaped Slabs	14****

	Name	Numbers
XIII.	Grooved Stones	13****
	A. plain transverse	1****
	B. crosshatched–incised transverse	1****
	C. longitudional–incised transverse	1****
	D. plain longitudional	1****
	E. narrow transverse	1****
	F. narrow longitudional	2****
	G. threaded	1****
XIV.	Celts[3]	76****
	A. chipped with polished bits	32****
	B. chipped with chipped bits	27****
	C. allover smoothed/polished	5****
XV.	Pendants	14****
XVI.	Discs	10****
XVII.	Beads	8****
XVIII.	Engraved and Punctated Stones	4****

[1]The counts of the pecked, ground, or polished stone tool types given in this table refer to, unless otherwise noted, only that half of the Cut 2 collection presently at Columbia University. It should be pointed out, however, that the descriptions in the text, in all cases, refer to the total collections from the cuts and the test trenches. A single asterisk * next to the count numbers indicates that the sub-type was found only on the surface of the site; two asterisks ** next to the count numbers indicate that the sub-type was found only in the Iraq Museum share of the Cut 2 collections; three asterisks *** indicate that the sub-type was found only in the Cut 1 collections; and four asterisks **** indicate the counts given include all specimens of the type or sub-type found at Zawi Chemi Shanidar (cuts, test trenches, and from surface).

[2]The counts given for the types include all specimens, whole and fragmentary, while the counts for the sub-types include only those specimens which could be positively classified. Therefore, the sub-type totals may not tally with the type totals.

[3]It was decided to include all these related tools under the classification "celts", even though some of them were made by chipping alone, without the use of pecking, grinding, or polishing techniques.

The Zawi Chemi period querns may be divided into the following sub-types: A. trough, B. flat, C. bifacial, and D. combination quern-motar.

IIA. *trough* (pl. 4e) – On the basis of present evidence these are closed trough querns. The troughs vary from very shallow ones, about 1.0 cm. in depth to ones as deep as 10.0 cm. with 6.0 cm. as an average trough depth. Possibly there should be a division of the trough querns into two varieties: those with a shallow trough (3.0 cm. and under) and those with a deeper trough (over 3.0 cm.). The deeper troughs may vary from V-shaped to a more open U-shaped one, with the shallower troughs naturally more open yet. The rim around the trough could either be left the smooth, natural rock surface, or it could also be pecked like the trough. The mullers must have been used in the querns with a rotary motion rather than with a back and forth motion. In the more V-shaped querns, furthermore, the mullers must have been used along the sides of the querns or at an angle to the base, for they could not fit in flat along the base of the trough. There are only three trough querns complete enough to be measured. There is an unusually large, ovate one which measures: 58 cm. in length, 33 cm. in width, 15 cm. in thickness, 5 cm. in depth of trough, and 39 cm. in length of trough. The second quern is roughly rectangular shaped with a broad shallow trough; it measures 38 cm. in length, 22.5 cm. in width, and the trough is 2 cm. deep. The third specimen, probably an ovate quern, measures 47 cm. in length, 29 cm. in width, and 12.5 cm. in thickness. The fragmentary querns which could be measured range from 19 to 25 cm. in width.

IIB. *flat* (pl. 4f,g) – This sub-type is obviously less common at Zawi Chemi than the trough querns (see Table 4) just described. It is, however, more characteristic of the coeval occupation at Shanidar Cave, perhaps suggesting some seasonal functional use. Generally the flat querns seem to be smaller sized than the trough querns, and have flat pecked working surfaces. The one illustrated in pl. 4f is 18 cm. wide and was probably about 35 cm. long. It is only 6 cm. thick. The pecked working area is across the entire width of the specimen; there is no rim as in the trough querns. The larger quern shown in pl. 4g was found in Cut 1. It measures ca. 47 cm. in length, ca. 30 cm. in width, and 12.5 cm. in thickness. The flat upper surface has a pecked ovate area outlined on it, but a trough has not yet been formed on it. Perhaps this specimen should be viewed as an unfinished trough quern; i.e., the trough has been outlined but not as yet pecked out.

IIC. *bifacial* – There is only one such quern from Zawi Chemi Shanidar, found on the surface of the site. It is a fragmentary specimen, but it seems to have a trough on both surfaces. One trough is 3 cm. deep and the other is 2 cm. deep.

IID. *combination quern-mortar* (pl. 4h,i) – These are basically large trough querns, with a small circular hole in the base of the trough. The troughs were pecked to shape and then the hole fashioned in the trough. Although none of these querns is complete, the following measurements could be made: 28.6 and 30.0 cm. in quern width; 17.0, 18.0 and 19.3 cm. in trough width; 5.0 to 12.0 cm. in trough depth (in 10 specimens); and 1.5 to 8.0 cm. in hole depth (in 13 examples). In the four examples where it was measured, the diameter of the hole is 7.5, 7.9, 8.0, and 8.0 cm., really quite uniform measurements. Possibly this quern sub-type was used like a hopper, to keep the pounded kernels from being dispersed.

III. *Mortar* (pl. 4j) – Although only one mortar has been found in the excavations at Zawi Chemi Shanidar, and that one unfortunately from a disturbed context, I still feel that mortars were used by the Zawi Chemi period people. The single known example is a large, deep boulder mortar, made out of the same quartzite rock used for the querns, and fashioned by the same techniques used to make the querns. It should also be noted here that large numbers of pestle-like stone objects were recovered from the Zawi Chemi period deposits (described below). Three boulder mortars were picked up on the surface of Zawi Chemi Shanidar.

IV. *Bowl* (pl. 4k) – A single, fragmentary example of what may have been a large (ca. 30.0 cm. in diameter) shallow, roughly circular stone bowl was found in the excavations in a Layer A context. In material (quartzite) and technique of manufacture it resembles the Zawi Chemi period querns, and, therefore, I believe it belongs to the Layer B (Zawi Chemi) occupation. This piece has been pecked to shape on the outer or concave surface, with a definite flattened area at the base. The concave or interior surface of the bowl has a smooth finish which must have been purposely fashioned. It thus differs from the querns in surface finishing technique, suggesting that it must have been used differently.

V. *Abraders* (pl. 5a-f, and fig. 15a-c) – These are elongate stones used at the ends. The ends are smoothed and characteristically flattened, but they may be convex; presumably they were used for some sort of abrading or rubbing function. They may be sub-divided into the following five sub-types: A. pebble, B. large pebble, C. partly pecked, D. pecked, and E. combination abrader-pecking stone.

VA. *pebble* (pl. 5a,b, and fig. 15a,b) – These are made on cylindrical or irregular shaped pebbles, with little or no modification except for the ends, which are smoothed and flattened through use. In the two complete examples only one of the ends shows use wear. These two measure 9.0x5.9x4.7 cm. and 5.0x5.3x5.1 cm., but some of the broken ones must have been larger.

VB. *large pebble* (pl. 5c) – The two examples from Cut 2 are fragments of large, elongate pebbles with at least one smoothed convex end (other end missing), but otherwise with no shape modifications. The following measurements could be made: greater than 11.3 and 6.6 cm. in length; and 7.2 and 6.2 cm. in width.

VC. *partly pecked* (pl. 5d, and fig. 15c) – These are elongate stones with straight, smoothed ends and partly or extensively pecked sides. The upper and lower surfaces which may be flattish or convex, can have a little pecking but for the most part are unmodified. All the examples are broken, but they range in width from 3.1 to 8.0 cm. and were larger than 12.3 cm. in length.

VD. *pecked* (pl. 5e) – These are elongated cylindrical stones, pecked all around their sides, and with straight, smoothed ends. All are broken, but the following measurements could be made: width ranges from 3.4 to 6.1 cm., and they could measure longer than 12.9 cm.

VE. *combination pebble abrader-pecking stone* (pl. 5f) – These are abraders which were also used at one end for pecking. The two measurable examples are 11.0x3.7 cm. and 14.6x5.1 cm.

VI. *Pounders* (pl. 5g) – These are large, elongate stones, resembling the abraders in shape, but with roughened or shattered ends rather than the smoothed ones characteristic of the abraders. The pounders are also more consistently made on large-sized stones, while the abraders are more variable in size. The pounders appear to have been used for crushing or pounding or other heavy work. In this sense they could be said to resemble the hammerstones. All examples present for study are from party pecked pounders (pl. 5g). They are elongate, largish stones in which part of the sides and the ends are pecked. The upper and lower surfaces (which are characteristically flattish) are not pecked, while one or both sides are pecked. All the specimens are broken, but they range in width from 4.9 to 7.2 cm., and may be greater than 15.7 cm. in length. Shaft fragments from all-round pecked specimens possibly belong to the pounder type.

VII. *Hammerstones* (pl. 5h-q) – Hammerstones occur in great numbers at Zawi Chemi Shanidar, in a variety of sub-types. They may be described under the following sub-types: A. simple, B. single pitted, C. double pitted, and D. greenstone.

VIIA. *simple* (pl. 5h-j) – These are made on various shapeu pebbles, but elongate or roughly circular or ovate pebbles seem to have been favored. The ends of these stones served as hammerstones as evidenced by heavy use wear. The smallest of the complete specimens measures 7.6x6.0 cm. and the largest 24.8xca. 12.0 cm. The latter specimen (pl. 5j) is a large, bi-convex, ovate cobble the tapered ends of which were used for battering; one of the surfaces also may have been used for abrading.

VIIB. *single pitted* (pl. 5k) – These hammerstones have a single deep pit on one of their surfaces. The two measurable specimens are 14.7x9.7 cm. and 10.8xca. 8.2 cm.

VIIC. *double pitted* (pl. 5l) – These have a single pit on each face, and hammering use wear on the ends. The two measured specimens are 11.3x7.9 cm. and 10.2x8.4 cm. An interesting tool from the Cut 2 collections stored in the Iraq Museum has a rough indentation on three of its sides; these may be due to use or they may have been made intentionally to notch the piece.

VIID. *greenstone* (pl. 5m-q) – These are made from specially selected stones, characteristically having a greenish or green-gray color with a lustrous look and a greasy feel. Some mottled or banded white and green or greenish-gray combinations also are present.

This is a common Zawi Chemi hammerstone sub-type and may be divided into the following three varieties on the basis of shape and use pattern: The variety VIID1 specimens are roughly discoidal in shape with flattish upper and lower surfaces (but sometimes plano-convex in section), and with hammerstone use wear all or almost all around the periphery (pl. 5m,n). Many of these tools are broken, but the complete ones range from 5.4x5.4 cm. to 7.8x8.8 cm. in size. The variety VIID2 specimens are roughly ovate in shape with hammerstone use characteristically limited to the ends (pl. 5o). They range in size from 6.3x6.6 cm. to 8.6x6.1 cm. The variety VIID3 specimens are roughly ball shaped hammerstones, used all over (pl. 5p,q). They range in size from 4.5x4.5 cm. to 6.6x5.3 cm.

VIII. *Pecking Stones* (pl. 6a-e, and fig. 15d-g) – These are variously shaped, smallish stones, usually of quartzite, used for pecking or light hammering. They may be divided into the following six sub-types: A. simple, B. elongate pebble, C. combination pecking stone-chopper, D. combination pecking stone-rubber, E. combination pecking stone-facetted rubber, and F. notched.

VIIIA. *simple* (pl. 6a,b, and fig. 15d) – These are rounded or ovate pebbles, used either at the ends or all around the periphery. The surfaces may be unmodified or may show some pecking or may rarely have very shallow pits. They range in size from 5.1x4.7 cm. to 10.5x9.0 cm.

VIIIB. *elongate pebble* (pl. 6c, and fig. 15e) – These are flattish, elongate pebbles the ends of which have been used for light hammering or pecking. They have not been purposely shaped. The two complete ones are 9.3x2.2 cm. and 10.9x3.8 cm., but one of the broken ones is from a larger sized tool.

VIIIC. *combination pecking stone-choppers* (pl. 6d, and fig. 15f) – These are small, flat, disc-like stones which were first pecked completely around the sides, and then used in such a way as to produce or require heavy bifacial flaking around the edges. Perhaps the flaking was due only to the heavy use, but some of it is so regular that purposeful shaping is suggested. In any event the working edges, in part or even almost completely become thinned from bifacial flaking, and this thinned edge apparently continued to be used for some purpose. Some of these tools also exhibit heavy abrasion striations on their flat surfaces. Such tools in the Columbia University Cut 2 collections range in size from 5.4x 5.3 cm. to 9.0x8.2 cm., but a larger one (10.8x8.7 cm.) is in the Iraq Museum collections.

VIIID. *combination pecking stone-rubbers* (pl. 6e, and fig. 15g) – These are usually flattish, ovate pebbles used for pecking at the ends and for rubbing on the faces. They range in size from 6.4x8.2 cm. to 8.3x7.6 cm. One of these tools appears to be double pitted.

VIIIE. *combination pecking stone-facetted rubber* – The one example of this sub-type is an ovate, flat pebble (measuring ca. 6.5x5.0 cm.), one end of which has been facetted straight across, and the other end and part of the sides used for pecking.

VIIIF. *notched* – These are flat, ovate pecking stones with opposite shallow side notches (along the long axis). The sides have been pecked all around and the surfaces show evidence of rubbing. The one measurable specimen is 7.6x9.1 cm.

IX. *Rubbers* (pl. 6f-m, and fig. 15h-j) – These are a characteristic Zawi Chemi tool type. They are small sized tools with distinctive rubbing use wear patterns. They may be divided into two sub-types: A. end facetted and B. plain.

IXA. *end facetted* (pl. 6f-l, and fig. 15h-j) – These distinctive tools are made on small, flattish pebbles, the ends and occasionally the sides of which have been facetted. They may be divided into three varieties on the basis of shape. The variety IXA1 specimens (pl. 6f-h, and fig. 15h) are narrow, elongate facetted rubbers in which the length is 3½ times or more greater than the width and one or both ends have been facetted. When an end has been rubbed from both sides that end becomes more-or-less pointed. These rubbers range from 5.0x1.3 cm. to 10.2x2.1 cm. in size. The variety IXA2 specimens are broad elongate facetted rubbers in which the length varies from 1½ to 3 times the width (pl. 6i, and fig. 15i). Except for this proportional shape difference, these rubbers are identical to those in the above variety. They range in size from 4.3x2.7 to 9.0x3.4 cm. The variety IXA3 specimens are circular or ovate facetted rubbers, exhibiting several different use wear patterns (pl. 6j-l, and fig. 15j). The IXA3 facetted rubbers in the Columbia University Cut 2 collections range in size from 3.6x5.2 cm. to 5.4x6.2 cm., but slightly smaller and larger ones are present in the Iraq Museum collections.

IXB. *plain* (pl. 6m) – These are small, flat pebbles, usually ovate, with rubbing use wear on one or both surfaces. The ones in the Cut 2 Columbia University collection range in size from 4.3x3.4 cm. to 6.3x4.8 cm. but one in the Iraq Museum collection is 7.7x6.5 cm.

X. *Rings* (pl. 6n) – Of the four stone rings found at Zawi Chemi Shanidar only one was found in a layer B (Zawi Chemi period) context. However, because of the stone selected and the technique of manufacture used I believe the rings belong to the Zawi Chemi period occupation. They have been pecked all over to shape, and three of them are circular and one is ovate. The central hole has been drilled from both surfaces, giving it a biconical section. The hole is much larger on the surface of the ring than in the center of the shaft; in the two specimens where measurements could be made the shafts are 5.0 and 4.0 cm. at the surface and only 2.0 cm. inside the shaft. The stone rings measure in overall size 9.6x9.5 cm. and 9.7x10.0 cm.

XI. *Cupped Stones* (pl. 6o) – These resemble the pitted mullers, but have deep depressions or cups on both faces rather than shallow pits. One is definitely circular in shape and one seems to be ovate; the third is too fragmentary to permit shape determination. The cups have been pecked from both faces and in two of them a distance of 1.5 and 2.0 cm. separates them, but in the third example only ca. 0.7 cm. separates the two cups. The circular specimen measures 11.0x11.4 cm. and the pits measure ca. 4.7 cm. in diameter and are ca. 1.0 cm. deep. The ovate shaped specimen measures ca. 11.8x11.0 cm. and the diameter of the cups is 2.8 cm. This latter specimen has lightly pecked sides but the top and bottom faces are not worked. The two others appear to have been pecked all over and to show heavy use wear. The function of these well made and shaped stones is not known, although they do resemble the pitted mullers. The two specimens with use wear could not have been unfinished stone rings, but possibly the ovate specimen was just that.

XII. *Shaped Slabs* (pl. 6p) – These are large, flat, sandstone discs, usually circular or more rarely sub-rectangular in shape. The one illustrated in pl. 6p (sub-rectangular shaped) measures 28.5x32.0 cm. and ranges from 1.4 to 2.2 cm. in thickness. The other discs are ca. 35.0 cm. in diameter and range from 1.3 to 3.8 cm. in thickness. The surfaces of the discs are characteristically grainy and rough, and most of them show traces of heating.

XIII. *Grooved Stones* (pl. 6q-w) – A typological analysis and a functional study of these Zawi Chemi tools have already been published (Solecki and Solecki, 1970), along with a laboratory report of the stones themselves (Drew, in Solecki and Solecki, 1970). A summary of these findings will be presented here. The grooved stone tools are made from chlorite or related minerals, materials which resemble steatite. Dr. Drew (in Solecki and Solecki, 1970, p. 840) has noted in fact that black steatite cannot be distinguished from black chlorite, without reference to an x-ray diffraction test. Chlorite is a soft mineral, and a fairly heat resistant one. Dr. Drew (in Solecki and Solecki, 1970, pp. 839-840) reported that the Zawi Chemi specimens she studied showed evidence of heating.

The Zawi Chemi people fashioned chunks of chlorite into these grooved tools, as well as other objects (e.g., beads). The stones were ground to shape and the surfaces are usually covered with striation marks from the final smoothing. The surfaces also often have a greasy feel or luster. The grooves may be narrow or broad (as described below), reflecting different usages. The broad grooves may be highly polished or have incised surfaces (crosshatched or lineal) again reflecting different functions. Seven grooved stone sub-types may be outlined for the Zawi Chemi collection: A. plain transverse, B. crosshatched-incised transverse, C. longitudional-incised transverse, D. plain longitudional, E. narrow transverse, F. narrow longitudional, and G. threaded. It should be noted here that the plain transverse subtype (XIIIA) is by far the most common with six examples, followed by the narrow longitudional sub-type (XIIIE) with two examples; the other sub-types are all represented by only a single example.

XIIIA. *plain transverse* (pl. 6q) – These are roughly ovate in shape with one flat and one highly convex face. A deep, polished groove is present on the convex face of each piece, across the short axis, approximately in the center. All of the examples are broken, but the following dimensions could be determined. They range in length from 5.2 to 7.1 cm., the one width measurement is 3.7 cm., and in thickness the range is 2.5 to 4.2 cm. The grooves are from 1.1 to 1.6 cm. wide and 0.7 to 1.1 cm. deep.

XIIIB. *crosshatched-incised transverse* (pl. 6r) – The one example is an ovate, plano-convex stone with one broad and one pointed end. It is small sized, measuring 3.6 cm. long, 2.3 cm. wide, and 1.6 cm. in thickness. The groove runs across the entire width of the convex face and is 1.1 cm. across and 0.5 cm. deep. A grid is incised in the groove, formed by five lines parallel to the short axis and seven parallel to the long axis. There are also several shallow incisions and a single deep one between the groove and the broad end of the piece.

XIIIC. *longitudional-incised transverse* (pl. 6s) – The one example is a small, roughly rectangular stone, 3.1 cm. long, 2.0 cm. wide, and 1.3 cm. thick. The groove has been cut almost to the full size of the specimen, to a depth of 0.5 cm. Nine parallel lines are deeply incised along the length of the groove.

XIIID. *plain longitudional* (pl. 6t) – Again only one example of this sub-type has been found at Zawi Chemi Shanidar. It is a thick, ovate stone, with a flattened base and rounded sides. It measures 7.2 cm. in length, 4.7 cm. in width, and 4.2 cm. in thickness. The single groove cut longitudionally into the top surface is highly polished and measures 1.2 cm. across and 0.7 cm. deep.

XIIIE. *narrow transverse* (pl. 6u) – Again only one example of this sub-type has been found at Zawi Chemi Shanidar. It is ovate shaped with both ends flattened, and plano-convex in section. It measures 5.5 cm. in length, 4.3 cm. in width, and 2.8 cm. in thickness. Two narrow but deep grooves are cut transversely across the top face. These grooves taper towards the sides; in the center of the piece they measure 0.4 and 0.5 cm. across. There is another deep, narrow groove cut diagonally across one of the ends of the specimen.

XIIIF. *narrow longitudional* (pl. 6v) – One (pl. 6v) is a small, roughly ovate, plano-convex broken specimen, on the flat surface of which are six or perhaps seven parallel, narrow longitudional grooves. It measures 2.3 cm. in width, 1.4 cm. in thickness, and was more than 3.2 cm. long. The second example is also broken, but was a considerably larger piece; it measures 3.8 cm. in width, 2.3 cm. in thickness, and was more than 6.6 cm. in length. It is plano-convex in section and the flat surface has sixteen parallel narrow longitudional grooves. The convex face also seems to have the remains of a broad groove.

XIIIG. *threaded* (pl. 6w) – The one specimen placed in this sub-type is really an unique object. It is a roughly elongate rectangular, box-shaped stone, with four right angled sides, but with irregular ends. One side has two channel grooves cut in such a way that the grooves have a threaded appearance; they also show use wear. The two other sides of this specimen each have a single roughly circular depression.

The reason for such a variety of grooved stone sub-types in the Zawi Chemi culture is some-what of a puzzle, but presumably each served a different function – for a specialized technique or for use with a distinct type of material (e.g. reeds, wood, bone, etc.). The conclusions of the functional study of the grooved stones found in Solecki and Solecki (1970) may be summarized as follows. The plain transverse (XIIIA) and the longitudional (XIIID) sub-types were probably used for straightening cane shafts, involving a heating process. The cross-hatched (XIIIB) and longitudional (XIIIC) incised transverse ones may have been used for the smoothing of wood or bone shafts or other objects (e.g. bone beads). The irregular surfaces created by the incisions would have made such functions possible. The narrow longitudional grooved specimens (XIIIF), with their rough surfaces, also might have been used for the smoothing of bone or wooden objects. The unique specimen with the threaded channel grooves (XIIIG) might have been used in the manufacture of narrow bone shafts, and possibly also the narrow transverse grooved stones (XIIIE).

XIV. *Celts* (pl. 7, and fig. 16a-g) – A celt is according to the dictionary definitions: "A primitive chisel or ax-shaped stone or metal implement," (Webster, 1948, p. 163), or "An ax of stone or metal without perforation or groove for hafting" (American College Dictionary, 1967, p. 194). Archaeologists have used the term for a number of different tools. Sonnenfeld (1962, pp. 56-65) in his study of some three hundred New World stone celts or celt-like tools (both chipped and ground) finds such uses as the following attributed to them: hafted and unhafted axes, adzes, hatchets, choppers, chisels, wedges, scrapers, hoes, spades, picks and flakers. We know from ethnographic records that some have ceremonial significance rather than a practical function. There is, therefore, evident confusion as to exactly what is meant by a celt in the archaeological literature.

The earliest celt-like tools are found during the Proto-Neolithic period and become important tools during the Neolithic. As Cole (1957, pp. 495-519) has pointed out they must have been important to Neolithic man for he chose special stone for them, made them with care, and must have spent many man hours fashioning them. They are evidently important in wood-working cultures, and must have been used by these early agriculturalists to clear their lands to make wooden utensils from the felled trees.

The celts from Zawi Chemi were made out of specially selected stones, shaped into the desired forms by chipping alone or by a combination of chipping and grinding/polishing techniques. Only rarely in the Zawi Chemi collection do we find the celt surface roughly smoothed/polished allover, a type that was to become common in the later Neolithic period. The Zawi Chemi celts were not grooved or perforated, so the determination of their precise hafted positions and functions presents some problems. We may in fact be dealing with at least five different types of tools in this collection: axes, adzes, gouges, chisels, and wedges. Perhaps we should here define exactly what we mean by these five tool types.

The axe according to Webster (1948, p. 75) is "A cutting tool for felling trees, and chopping, splitting, or hewing wood. It consists of an edged head fixed to a handle, the edge or edges being parallel to the handle." Cole (1957, pp. 505-506) in her discussion of the axe notes that it has the following characteristics: the edge is parallel to the handle; it is mounted in a handle or vice-versa; it is equal faced and symmetrically edged; is used to drive into wood and to split it; was thick to carry weight and bear shock; and is mainly for clearing forests. We are willing to go along generally with Cole's list of specialized axe traits, but would like to point out that modern types of axes exist that do not fit her definition. The early colonists in North America were faced with a world of forests which they had to cut down to make their settlements; and the wood from which, incidentally, they used for their houses, their fuel, their furniture, and much of their equipment. Early tool catalogs had a great variety of specialized axes, and more than fifty patterns of axe heads alone were listed (Sloane, 1974, p. 12). For example, the most essential Early American tool was the chisel-edged axe, for hewing rather than felling (Sloane, 1974, pp. 14-15). This axe of course does not have a symmetrical bit, but it was mounted like an axe and used like an axe, not an adze. It was a kind of plane or striking chisel used by the colonists for hewing round logs into square beams. And then the mortise axes looked like chisels but were mounted like axes and were pounded on their heads to make square holes for tenons (Sloane, 1974, p. 12). The axes with symmetrical bits were for felling trees. So axes are used for felling trees and for shaping the downed trees into useful objects. Axes are particularly important in cultures which have to deal with clearing large forested tracts. They are heavy tools, fixed into a handle with the cutting edge parallel to the handle. For ordinary felling the bits were broad and symmetrical, but for specialized jobs the bit could be otherwise shaped.

An adze according to the dictionary definition (Webster, 1948, p. 17) is "A cutting tool having a thin arching blade set at right angles to the handle." Cole (1957, pp. 505-506) notes that the adze has the following characteristics: is generally bound on to a handle; has the edge across the handle; has one face longer and flatter; and is usually ground on one side. She notes that it is thinner than the axe as its momentum was less important. She notes that the adze is for tilling the soil or to hew out canoes and construct wheels (Cole, 1957, p. 505). So the adze is a sharp-edged tool with assymetric bitted blade, hafted at right angles to the handle (as opposed to the axe in which the blade is parallel to the handle); lighter in weight than the axe; and used in different ways and for different purposes than the axe. The bits of modern adzes are all beveled on the inside (or towards the handle) and presumably the ancient ones were hafted the same way, for practical reasons.

Chisels and gouges are related tools. According to the dictionary definition the chisel is (Webster, 1948, p. 176) "A metal tool with cutting edge at the end of a blade, used in dressing, shaping, or otherwise working timber, stone, etc." and a gouge is (Webster, 1948, p. 431)

"A kind of chisel with a concave-convex cross-section." Today there are many kinds of chisels (Sloane, 1974, p. 52). The basic wood chisels perform many tasks but the main one is to chisel or cut out superfluous wood. They usually have short wooden handles, but unhafted ones do occur. Some specialized chisels were designed not for striking but to be used with two hands. Chisels have asymmetric or beveled ends. The gouge as indicated above is a type of chisel with a concave or hollow working edge, used in much the same way as the chisel. The term gouge has been used in the archaeological literature for tools that were probably not mounted or used like modern gouges. The Khartoum Neolithic gouges are such an example (Arkell, 1953, pp. 31-32), and Arkell (1953, p. 31) notes that these gouges were "...really a form of hollow-cut adze and not really a gouge at all. ...It is to be presumed that these gouges, or rather adzes, were used for hollowing tree-trunks to make dug-out canoes as are still used on the White Nile..."

The wedge, according to the dictionary definition (Webster, 1948, p. 1142) is "A piece of wood, metal, etc., tapering to a thin edge, used in splitting wood, rocks, etc., in raising heavy bodies, and the like."

Now that these basic tool types have been defined, I think we can return to a discussion of the term "celt" as used in this report, and its general value to the prehistorian. The usefulness of the term is its very vagueness of meaning. We don't know how most of these tools were hafted or how they were used, and to definitely call them axes, adzes, wedges, chisels or gouges, etc. can not only be misleading but also sometimes may be wrong. Therefore, we shall describe this entire group of Zawi Chemi tools under the general term "celt", dividing them into three sub-types: A. chipped celts with polished bits, B. chipped celts with chipped bits, and C. celts allover smoothed/polished. After a general discussion of these three broad sub-types based on the entire Zawi Chemi celt collection, we shall try to determine something about the various functions of these tools and something about possible hafting techniques, based primarily on an intensive study of that part of the Cut 2 celt collection presently available for study in the Columbia University collections. Pertinent materials from the other half of Cut 2, from Cut 1, and test trenches will also be included.

Celts are found in fair numbers towards the top of the Zawi Chemi cultural deposits. The sixty-two celts found in Cut 2 have the following stratigraphic distribution:

Level	Numbers
0 – .25 meters	0
.25 – .50 meters	2
.50 – .75 meters	55
.75 – 1.00 meters	4
1.00 – 1.25 meters	1
1.25 – 1.50 meters	0
total	62

On the basis of the above figures it seems evident that celts came into popularity at the site sometime after the Zawi Chemi culture became established there. Just about ninety percent of of the celts were found in the .50-.75m. level and the one celt from the 1.00-1.25 m. level came from a disturbed area which also contained pottery. Celts also were rather common on the surface of the site, brought up by modern plowing; nineteen were found in the surface collections.

The Zawi Chemi celts were made of specially selected materials, a favorite being a mottled green colored stone. The three broad sub-types of celts may be described as follows:

XIVA. *chipped celts with polished bits* (pl. 7a-g, and fig. 16a-c) – These are the most numerous celt sub-type. They are shaped by chipping and then the bits were sharpened by grinding and polishing. Final shaping could be done by chipping after the polished bit was fashioned, primarily along the sides. These celts tend to be roughly rectangular shaped but more ovate ones and even a discoid one is present; waisting of the sides, apparently for hafting, is also known.

The bit, characteristically symmetrically polished from both faces, extends up from the working edge for from two to five centimeters. The use wear pattern evident on the bits could be either symmetric or assymetric. The rest of the tool is either the original cortex surface of the stone or is a chipped surface. The celts show evidence of heavy use wear and some or even most of the polished bit surface may be gone. The butts may be nicely thinned (apparently for hafting); thinned by battering; or heavy and thick, both plain and battered. At least some of the battered ones were probably never hafted, and suggest a specialized function.

The shape of the bits and the butts and the use wear patterns evident on them, suggest that these celts could have been used as axes, adzes, chisels, and possibly even wedges. A further discussion of celt function is given below.

XIVB. *chipped celts with chipped bits* (pl. 7h-l, and fig. 16d-f) – These also occur with frequency at Zawi Chemi Shanidar. These celts today have no evidence of polishing and it appears that the general shaping as well as the forming of the bit was exclusively done by chipping, but it must be pointed out that perhaps some of them originally had polished bits which were lost through extensive use. Again these celts tend to be roughly rectangular in shape, but may be more ovate, and even a triangular one is present. There is some waisting of the sides. The chipped celts with chipped bits in the Cut 2 collection available for study have assymetric shaped bits but symmetric bits may be present in the other Zawi Chemi samples. Butts may be thin or thick.

Generally, these celts are more roughly fashioned than those in sub-type XIVA, and seem to have been heavy duty tools. From our evidence they could have been used as adzes (most common), gouges, or even as a pick.

XIVC. *allover smoothed/polished* (pl. 7m,n, and fig. 16g) – These celts are more neatly shaped and have extensive areas of smoothing/polish. One such celt (pl. 7m and fig. 16g) was found in the .50-.75 m. level of Cut 2 and four were found on the surface of the site.

They are roughly elongated ovates in shape, with one end noticeably narrower than the other. The celts show some smoothing/polish over much of their surface, but a totally regular surface was not achieved. Surface depressions and irregularities are still present. At least one of them still shows evidence of side chipping for shaping. It seems likely that these celts were hafted and used as axes.

The Cut 2 celts in the Columbia University collections were intensively studied to determine typological variations and the possible functional significances of these variations. Unique pieces from the other Zawi Chemi collections were also included when pertinent. The descriptions below are based on these studies.

Within the first sub-type, chipped celts with polished bits (XIVA), we can determine the following varieties:

XIVA1. celts with polished bits and neatly thinned butts (pl. 7a) – The one specimen is a thinnish delicate celt, roughly rectangular shaped but with convex sides. The butt end has been carefully thinned by chipping, probably for hafting. The bit is symmetrical in section but is worn assymetrically, i.e., the wear is primarily from one face. The use wear pattern and the thinness of the piece suggests that it might have been used as an adze rather than an axe, even though it has a symmetric bit.

XIVA2. celts with polished bits and battered thinned butts (pl. 7b, and fig. 16a) – The one specimen is a thick, heavy, rectangular shaped celt, with slightly concave sides (waisted). The butt end is quite thin but shows evidence of heavy battering. It could not be determined if this thinning was for the purpose of hafting or as a consequence of use battering. The bit is symmetrical in section and shows use on both faces. The weight, shape and use wear pattern of the bit suggest that this celt was used as an axe.

XIVA3. celts with polished bits and battered butts (pl. 7c) – The example available for study is a short, thick, ovate shaped celt, almost triangular in section, with a sharply thinned bit and a thick, battered butt. The bit is symmetric and shows heavy use from both faces. The small size and relative thickness of the piece; the shape and wear pattern on the bit; and the shape and wear pattern on the butt suggest that this celt may have been used as a wedge or a chisel.

XIVA4. celts with polished bits and very thick butts (pl. 7d, and fig. 16b) – The one specimen is a large, thick celt with a highly polished, symmetric bit (with no use wear), and a thick butt end (with extensive cortex area). Possibly this is an unfinished or unused specimen.

XIVA5. celts with polished bits and flat, truncated butts (pl. 7e) – These are medium-sized, roughly rectangular pieces. An interesting feature is that a large flake has been removed from along one of the sides on one of the faces; probably this feature is somehow related to hafting. The bits are polished symmetric and the one heavily used specimen has use evidence on both faces. The butts have been so prepared that they are flat across. Probably these were used as axes.

XIVA6. thin, flattish, disc-like celt with polished bit and thinned, chipped but (pl. 7f, and fig. 16c) – The bit has been polished from both faces but heavy use wear is present on only one face. The shape of this celt, plus the type of use wear suggests that it was used as an adze.

XIVA7. narrow, elongate, parallel sided celt with a highly polished rounded bit (pl. 7g) – The one example is made of a distinctive green stone and was chipped to shape and then polished at the bit and up a narrow central strip on one face. The piece is biconvex in section, but with one face noticeably more convex than the other. It is thick towards the butt end but tapers in section to a thinned and rounded polished bit. Small chips have been removed from the bit on both faces, apparently through use. The function of this tool is difficult to determine, especially as the butt end is missing. The thinness and narrowness of the bit rather eliminates use as an axe or an adze, and suggests some sort of chisel.

Within the sub-type, chipped celts with chipped bits (XIVB), we can determine the following varieties:

XIVB1. celts with chipped bits and chipped thinned butts (pl. 7h, and fig. 16d) – The one specimen is roughly elongate ovate in shape, plano-convex in section; with a broad bit and a tapering butt. The bit has been shaped from both faces but seems to have been primarily used on only the flatter face. Again the sides seem to have been purposely waisted. The use pattern suggests that this was an adze.

XIVB2. celts with chipped bits and flat, truncated butts (pl. 7i, and fig. 16e) – There is one good example and one possible example of this variety. These are thick, crude celts, with rounded, broadish bits, flaked sides (the good example seems to be waisted), and thick flattish butts. The bits have been flaked from both surfaces, but in such a way that there is one flat and one convex surface. This suggests that they were used as adzes.

XIVB3. chipped celts with chipped concave bits (pl. 7j) – These are crude tools, roughly worked. One end has been unifacially chipped to form what looks like a concave working edge. One side is a flat surface (possibly a hand hold) while the other side is roughly chipped. It is here suggested that these may be gouges.

XIVB4. unifacially chipped celts with chipped bits (pl. 7k) – In this variety the sides and one face have been chipped to shape the piece, while the other face is a smooth surface, more or less flat or convex, unmodified natural rock surface or only lightly smoothed and/or polished. The bit is chipped not polished. Such a celt (pl. 7k) found on the surface is large sized, with the smooth surface flattish but slightly incurving towards the bit and the chipped surface highly convex. The two surfaces converge to form a sharply thinned but broad U-shaped bit. The specimen appears to have been used as an adze.

XIVB5. triangular shaped chipped celt with pointed bit (pl. 7l, and fig. 16f) – The one example is plano-convex (roughly trapezoidal in section), with a large central cortex area on one face. It has been chipped to shape from the non-cortex face. The sides converge to a point at the bit end, while the butt end, although broadish, is considerably thinned.

The third celt sub-type (XIVC), celts allover smoothed/polished (pl. 7m,n, and fig. 15g), could not be divided into varieties on the basis of the small sample available for study. They probably were used as axes.

XV. *Pendants* (pl. 8a-j, fig. 15k-m) – The most characteristic Zawi Chemi pendant type is made on a flat, ovate marble disc and has two holes for suspension at one end (pl. 8a-d, and fig. 15k,m). One has a simple lineal incised decoration, but the others are undecorated. The two complete examples measure 3.8x3.1 cm. and 3.9x3.1 cm., but one of the broken ones was more than 5.4 cm. long. The broken piece illustrated in pl. 8d and fig. 15m may be a double holed pendant in the process of manufacture. It is a small, flat disc, ovate shaped, and made of a banded black-gray stone. Two small holes are drilled a short way into the piece, from one face, possibly representing suspension holes never completed. Including the last described specimen, there are seven double holed pendants in the Zawi Chemi collections. Then there are two thick, elongate-ovate (sinker like), single holed pendants (pl. 8e,g). One (pl. 8g) is of marble and was found on the surface of the site and the other (pl. 8e) is made of a banded gray-black rock and came from the excavations. The former measured 5.7x3.0 cm. and the latter 5.4x1.7 cm. Five other single holed stone pendants are present also. One is a large, flat, irregular shaped sandstone pendant (7.2x4.5 cm.) found on the surface of the site. Another (pl. 8f) is a large (4.8x4.2 cm.), flat, roughly ovate pendant. Apparently a natural pebble was used, with only little shaping at the more pointed end to make this pendant. A single hole, drilled from both faces, is in the approximate center of the piece. The specimen illustrated in pl. 8i has been fashioned into a thin, roughly trapezoidal shaped pendant, measuring 3.5x1.8 cm. A fourth pendant (pl. 8h, and fig. 15l) is fragmentary, but it obviously was a flat, narrow, elongate pendant with a single hold at the narrow end. The fifth specimen (pl. 8j) is broken but seems to have been a flat piece, tapering at the one remaining end, with straight parallel sides (not unlike the pendant in pl. 8h). A single hole has been drilled all the way through just below the end; and two holes drilled only partly through are below the suspension hole.

XVI. *Discs* (pl. 8o-q, and fig. 15o) – These are flat, ovate or circular discs, which have been ground to shape, with thinned or steep edges. The sides and/or the surfaces of these discs may show modification. Ten such specimens are in the Zawi Chemi collections; all but one which looks like sandstone are of marble. They may be blanks for the double holed pendants, for they are the correct size and shape for them. The measurable ones range in size from 2.3x1.9 to 5.0x4.0 cm., but one of the broken ones is from a larger specimen. It should be noted that a number of unworked discs (of marble and other materials) similar in shape and size also occur in the Zawi Chemi deposits, but these are naturally smoothed or polished discs, unshaped by man.

XVII. *Beads* (pl. 8k-m, and fig. 15n) – Eight stone beads have been found at Zawi Chemi Shanidar, certainly not a very large number. Five of these are made of chlorite. One is a large barrel shaped bead (pl. 8l), 2.3x1.2 cm. in size. Four are thickish, medium sized rounded beads, usually made with one side noticeably larger than the other (pl. 8m, and fig. 15n). Then there are two identical small, very thin disc beads, with a small hole in the middle (pl. 8n); they measure 0.9x0.9 cm. and are only 0.2 cm. thick. There is also one tubular marble bead (pl. 8k). It is broken but measured 0.7 cm. in diameter and was more than 1.6 cm. long.

XVIII. *Engraved and punctated stones* (pl. 8r, and fig. 15p) – Each one of these is a unique piece, modified apparently for some specific function. There is a small (4.0x2.1 cm.) flat, elongate, naturally polished stone, one face of which seems to have been used as a rubber and which has in addition three tiny punctations in a row at one end. Then there is a small (2.8x2.6 cm.) disc shaped piece of "mudstone" with a V-cut on one face. It could not be determined if the V-cut was accidentally or purposefully done. Then there is a fragment of an elongate stone with a single line incised across the width. Another specimen classified here and perhaps the most interesting one, is the one shown in pl. 8r, and fig. 15p. This is a small flattish, elliptical pebble, now split in half, with thin lines engraved on its one remaining surface. The line pattern that could be determined is as follows: 15 lines definitely go completely across the width; 8 lines probably go across the width but this is not certain because of the breakage; 3 lines go partly across the width and join one of the major lines listed above; 3 lines go partly across the width; and 4 lines go partly down the length of the piece. The last are found only along one side, are less deeply incised than the widthwise lines, and cut across the widthwise lines. The function of this piece is open to speculation. It has been suggested that it might be a tallying record of some sort, and maybe it was. But it also has been rubbed or abraded, for the central portion of the piece shows much use wear and in some instances the lines have been obliterated.

5.3. Flaked Stone Industry

The tools classified here may be divided into four distinct types (see Table 5). In the case of the spall tools and the flake knives a naturally sharp edge was produced by the very process of flaking. In the case of the choppers and the chisels a series of flakes were removed from an edge to form the desired tool. These tools are all relatively simple and roughly made, but their numbers indicate that they, espcially the spall tools which occur in truly impressive numbers, were important in the Zawi Chemi culture.

I. *Choppers* (pl. 9a-i) – Choppers occur in numbers at Zawi Chemi Shanidar. They may be divided into the following sub-types: A. pebble-unifacial, B. pebble-bifacial, C. flat pebble-unifacial, D. flat pebble-bifacial, E. single pitted, F. double pitted, G. all-around, H. pitted chopper-hammerstone, I. pebble chopper-hammerstone, J. chopper-muller, and K. flake or spall choppers.

IA. *pebble-unifacial* (pl. 9a) – These are suitably sized pebbles, one end of which has been fashioned into a chopper by flaking from one face. The flaking can extend up the sides as well. The other end is usually the unmodified pebble, and makes a good hand hold; rarely it may show some use wear. These choppers range in size from 7.9x7.7 cm. to 15.0x11.9 cm. and are from 3.7 to 5.2 cm. thick.

TABLE 5

Inventory of Flaked Stone Tools[1]

Name	Numbers
I. Choppers	45
A. pebble-unifacial	7
B. pebble-bifacial	6
C. flat pebble-unifacial	1
D. flat pebble-bifacial	8
E. single pitted	1
F. double pitted	1
G. all-around	4
H. pitted chopper-hammerstones	2
I. pebble chopper-hammerstone	1
J. chopper-muller	1
K. flake or spall choppers	13
II. Spall Tools	251
III. Chisels	13
A. light duty	8
B. heavy duty	5
IV. Flake Knives	11

[1]The counts of the flaked stone tool types given in this table refer to only that half of the Cut 2 collection presently at Columbia University.

IB. *pebble-bifacial* (pl. 9b) – These are suitably sized pebbles, one end of which has been fashioned into a chopper by flaking from both faces. The flaking is noticeably heavier on one face than the other, and may extend up the sides as well. The non-working end is unmodified, and forms a good hand hold. These choppers range in size from 8.2x7.3 cm. to 10.7x10.0 cm., and in thickness from 1.8x3.4 cm.

IC. *flat pebble-unifacial* – The single example available for study is a flat ovate chopper, flaked from only one face, measuring 4.2x7.9 cm.

ID. *flat pebble-bifacial* (pl. 9c) – These are flat pebbles, characteristically ovate in shape, flaked from both faces somewhere around their circumference. Some resemble the simple pecking stones (VIIIA) in shape and may even have some little pecking retouch, but those specimens classified here have extensive flake removal. These choppers range from 8.3x6.9 cm. to 11.8x8.5 cm. in size and in thickness from 1.9 to 3.4 cm.

IE. *single pitted* (pl. 9d) – The one example is a bifacially flaked chopper with a single deep pit on one face (the less heavily flaked face). This chopper measures 9.4x8.5 cm.

IF. *double pitted* (pl. 9e) – The single specimen available for study resembles the choppers in sub-type IB except that it has a deep pit on both faces. It was used as a chopper at one end and along one side and shows some hammering use, and both faces were used as rubbers. This chopper measures 6.9x8.2 cm.

IG. *all-around* (pl. 9f) – These are rough, chunky choppers flaked all-around their circumference. The ones in the Columbia University collection range in size from 10.2x9.0 to 13.2x11.6 cm., but smaller and larger ones are in the Iraq Museum collections.

IH. *pitted chopper-hammerstones* (pl. 9g) – One example (pl. 9g) is a double pitted pebble used as a unifacial chopper at one end and a hammerstone at the other end. It measures 10.0x9.3 cm. A second specimen is a pebble used as a chopper at one end and along one side and a hammerstone at the other end along one side. It has a single deep pit on one face; unfortunately, the other face is for the most part missing. A similar, definitely single pitted chopper-hammerstone is in the Iraq Museum Cut 2 collections.

II. *pebble chopper-hammerstone* (pl. 9h) – The one specimen available for study resembles the unifacial pebble choppers (IA), but here the end opposite the chopper shows hammering use wear. It measures 8.2x7.5 cm. Two similar but larger pebble chopper-hammerstones are in the Iraq Museum Cut 2 collections; one is a unifacial chopper and the other is bifacial.

IJ. *chopper-muller* – The one specimen looks like a double faced muller reused as a chopper around part of its circumference. It may be pitted on one face and measures 10.3x10.1 cm.

IK. *flake or spall choppers* (pl. 9i) – These are made on flakes, spalls, split pebbles, or occasionally on split tools, and are characteristically flaked from only one face. Some resemble the spall tools described below, and some are, in fact, reworked spall tools. These choppers are, however, distinguished from the spall tools by purposeful retouch flaking. These choppers range in size from 7.5x7.3 cm. to 15.7x13.3 cm.

II. *Spall Tools* (pl. 9j-o) – These are a most characteristic Zawi Chemi tool type; there are more than 250 of them in the Columbia University half of the Cut 2 collections. These are thin, broad, roughly elliptical shaped spalls with a sharp edge, produced without retouch through the flaking process. These spall tools fit nicely into the human hand and must have been used for some sort of cutting, scraping or chopping. They appear to have been primarily struck from large quartzite boulders or cobbles (pl. 9p) in a regular pattern. Some, however, were made by splitting pebbles, or even struck from such tools as mullers, hammerstones, pecking stones, or querns. They could have been used unmodified since, as noted above, they were detached in such a way that sharp broad working edges were automatically produced. The working edge usually is along the broad end of the tool, opposite the point where the spall was detached from the core. The two sides could also be used, and sometimes all four edges were used. A large proportion of the spall tools appear to have heavy use retouch, sometimes producing a beveled edge. These tools range in size from such small ones as 4.1x5.1 cm. or 3.9x4.9 cm. to large ones measuring 10.2x15.8 cm. or 11.2x15.0 cm.

A word should be said here about the spall cores (pl. 9p). These are the large quartzite cobbles or boulders from which most of the spall tools were detached. The spalls were removed from around the edges of the core, and only a part of the entire core circumference could be used. The spalls were removed from both faces. The two spall cores available for study measure 16.0x8.8 cm. and 23.5x28.0 cm., but both smaller and slightly larger ones were found at the site.

III. *Chisels* (pl. 9q,r, and fig. 16h,i) – The tools classified here have at least one broad, thinned end (created by flaking from both faces). The chisel ends are usually roughly straight across but they may be transverse. The chisels have been divided into two sub-types on the basis of function related to size: A. light duty and B. heavy duty.

IIIA. *light duty* (fig. 16h,i) – These may be made on small elongated pebbles (IIIA1) or small ovate or circular pebbles (IIIA2). The two examples of the first variety measure 8.3x 2.9 cm. and 5.8x2.3 cm. Only one of these is in good enough condition to study (fig. 16i). It has a single transverse working end flaked from both faces. The opposite end does not show any battering, suggesting this might be a hand held chisel of some sort. The other six light duty chisels are all of the IIIA2 variety (fig. 16h). Characteristically one end has a straight working edge (there is at least one diagonal example)flaked from both faces. In three of the specimens the opposite end has been battered and flaked, but in the other three the opposite end has been rubbed enough to form a weak facet and there is even some facetting evident at the chisel end. Again the function of these last described tools is obscure, as is the nature of the relationship, if any, between the rubbed edges and chisel ends. The IIIA2 chisels range in size from 4.5x3.4 cm. to 7.7x4.2 cm.

IIIB. *heavy duty* (pl. 9q,r) – These are made on pebbles, heavier and larger than those of sub-type IIIA. They range in size from 7.1x5.0 cm. to 10.4x7.7 cm. Three of them are made of the special greenstone characteristic of the sub-type VIID hammerstones. They all have one broad, bifacially thinned end and one battered end (variously used), suggesting heavy duty chisels. None of these specimens exhibit the rubbed facets of some of the light duty chisels, suggesting different functions.

IV. *Flake Knives* (pl. 9s) – There are a number of crude specimens, made out of a fine grained limestone in the form of thin flakes with roughly parallel sides. Now weathered and dull, but when first flaked they must have had sharp edges and were possibly used as knives. They range in size from 6.8x5.6 cm. to 8.5x2.4 cm.

5.4. Miscellany

The following miscellany recovered at Zawi Chemi Shanidar probably refers to the early occupation (Layer B): stones stained with hematite; lumps of lustrous taconite (pl. 8s,t); pieces of yellow and red ochre; fossil invertebrates (pl. 8u,v); pieces of stalagmite/stalagtite; a small quartz crystal; and bits of various minerals (e.g. aragonite, sidonite, or calcite).

5.5. Bone, Antler, Horn, and Ivory Industries

Bone tools and ornaments are characteristic of the Zawi Chemi culture. The bones of sheep and goat and the red deer were favored; e.g., such bones as the tibia and the metapodial and rarely a rib bone. Hollow bird bones also were used for beads, especially the tubular ones. At least six distinctive bone tool types were present, and bones were also used for hafts and for ornaments. Antlers and horns were also made into tools, and animal teeth perforated for beads. The Zawi Chemi people sometimes decorated their bone objects with simple designs made by carving, incising, or perforating.

5.5.1. Bone Industry

I. *Awls* (pl. 10a-e) – These are piercing tools of some sort with sharp pointed ends. They were common in the Zawi Chemi culture; eleven complete or almost complete ones were recovered, and there were about 150 awl fragments. The blunt end of the awl could be the unaltered articulation head, the altered articulation head, or the cut end of the bone. The awls are quite variable in size and shape. They could be long and slender with a long delicate point; squat and thick with a stout point; long and thick and with a stout point; or quite small in size. They vary in length from 6.0 cm. to 16.5 cm. Characteristically the points have concavo-convex shafts; the convex face is the inner bone surface and may have a spongy texture and the concave face is the original outer bone surface. Towards the point the shaft narrows and tends to become cylindrical in shape. In rare cases the shaft remains concavo-convex almost down to the tip, or occasionally the cylindrical part of the shaft may be quite long. Three or possibly four points lack the characteristic shaft shape and possibly were made on rib bones. They are flat, narrow, parallel sided tools, with prominent, all-over smoothing tracks. The one complete such specimen (pl. 10a) measures 14.4x0.8 cm., and has a cut butt end.

II. *Tools with polished, non-piercing ends* (pl. 10f-i) – Forty-five such tools were found at Zawi Chemi Shanidar, so they too were a characteristic bone tool type. The working ends are thinned, sometimes very much so, and rounded, chisel-like, or almost pointed in shape. The outstanding characteristic of these tools is that the working ends are highly polished on both faces for a short distance up from the tip, and usually tiny chips have been removed from the tip, apparently through use. They were made on split bones, and the articulation head may be left pretty much in tact, modified and perforated, or cut away. In the last instance the cut end is straight across or rounded. The complete specimens vary from 10.6 to 13.2 cm. in length, and the polished area at the working end varies from 1.2 to 2.3 cm. or 11 to 17% of the total length. The polished ends are bi-flat or bi-convex in section, but the shafts are concavo-convex. The concave faces of these tools have flat borders usually marked by transverse striations; these could be obliterated to various degress towards the working ends. In the more pointed specimens the concavity may go all the way down to the tip, thus considerably reducing the polished area on the concave face.

The functions of these tools is not known; they are so variable that they all could not have been used for the same purpose. They vary from quite thin and delicate to large, heavy, blunt-ended ones; and they form a continuum which could not be easily divided. Therefore, for convenience they are here all described together. The heavier ones may have been used in skin working, possibly as fat scrapers. The more delicate tools may have been used for some sort of matting, netting, or basketry. We do not have definite evidence of such industry at Zawi Chemi Shanidar, but there is evidence of simple matting from the coeval settlement at Shanidar Cave.

III. *Spatulas* (pl. 10j) – There are five examples of such tools in the Zawi Chemi collections, all broken. Four are end pieces and one is a shaft piece. They appear to resemble the above described bone tools in shape, but are much broader. The two specimens in which the width could be measured are 2.8 and 2.9 cm. wide, but one of the broken specimens was certainly much broader. They are made on split bones, and have a long, shallow channel groove with broad raised side borders on their split faces. Scratch marks are noticeable on the raised borders, even at the tip, which distinguishes them from the above tools which have polished tips. The outer or convex faces of the spatulas are polished. The ends of the spatulas may be broad and rounded or gently pointed. One of the spatulas has a simple lineal design incised on its outer surface, at the tip end.

IV. *Flat, pointed tools* (pl. 10k-m) – There are four definite specimens in the Zawi Chemi collections, all fragmentary. They are broad, flat tools, often perforated and/or decorated, with pointed or round-pointed ends. Although there are no complete ones from Zawi Chemi Shanidar, there are two similar complete tools from Shanidar Cave (pl. 11a). These are quite large tools (ca. 18.0 and 26.0 cm. long), both perforated at the blunt end. The Zawi Chemi examples are flat and shaped at the working end to a point or a rounded point. They lack the characteristic convavo-convex section of the awls and the non-piercing tools described above. They have been worked all-over, have obvious tool marks, and show evidence of polishing. Three out of the four specimens present have one or two perforations (1.8 to 3.8 cm. from the tip), and the fourth specimen is just a tiny tip end so it may have been perforated also. Two of these tools also have simple lineal incised decoration adjacent to the perforations.

There are two additional specimens which may belong to this type. They are very similar in shape and appearance to these tools, but they have a very slight concavity on their inner face. Even so they seem to belong to this tool type. Both have simple incised lineal decoration on their top face.

These tools were purposely shaped and carefully made by the Zawi Chemi people, but their function can only be guessed at. Again their shape and finish suggest that they were used in the manufacture of some sort of matting, netting, or basketry.

V. *Beveled ended tool* (pl. 10n) – There is only one example of this tool type. It was probably made on the distal end of a Cervus elaphus metapodial, and measures 11.0 cm. in length. The articulation head is smoothed but still recognizable, and there is a single perforation somewhat off center at the butt end. The specimen has been polished and has a simple lineal incised design. The working end is blunt and rounded, and has been beveled on the outside (dorsal) surface. Tiny flakes have been removed from the tip end through use.

VI. *Haft* (pl. 11b,c) – A single haft for the insertion of microliths was recovered at Zawi Chemi Shanidar. It is a flat, roughly crescent shaped specimen, measuring 21.7 cm. long, 2.4 cm. in greatest width, and 0.8 cm. in maximum thickness. It is smoothed all-over and appears to have been fashioned from an animal rib bone. There is a shallow wedge shaped groove along the entire concave side of the haft, deeper and wider at the ends than in the middle. It is presumed that microlithic blades were once fixed into the groove at both end portions of the haft, held in place by some sort of mastic. Probably the tool was held in the middle of the haft during use. It seems likely that the microliths were not inserted in that portion of the shaft because the groove was too shallow there. The piece resembles a sickle in shape, but it lacks the end handle found on roughly contemporary sickles in the area. Possibly it was used as a sickle, but surely it represents a cutting tool of some sort with a composite cutting edge.

VII. *Tiny points* (pl. 10o) – There are two such tiny points in the Zawi Chemi collections, measuring 1.8x0.4 cm. and 1.7x0.3 cm. They are blunt at one end and pointed at the other. In one, the blunt end is smoothed over and in the other the cutting marks are still evident. Probably associated with these tiny points are nineteen lenticular bone pieces with cut ends (pl. 10p). These are purposely shaped, elongated, narrow, lenticular pieces with sharply tapered ends. The two complete ones are 3.0x0.4 cm. and 3.3x0.5 cm. but a larger broken one is present. The ends have been cut off and blunted but not smoothed over or used in any way. It seems likely that these are waste pieces and that the cut off tips were the desired portions. From the shape of these pieces it appears probable that the tips were sharp pointed, suggesting that the tiny points described above came from such cores. It would have been very difficult if not impossible to have made such tiny points if they were not in the manufacturing process attached to larger pieces.

VIII. *Double-holed winged object* (pl. 10q) – There is only one such specimen; it is a highly polished, slightly plano-concave, winged object, measuring 3.8x1.3x0.35 cm. There are two holes drilled through the central portion of the object. There is a pair of lightly incised parallel lines through one of these holes on the flat face of the piece, as well as a series of light scratch marks between it and the other hole. The piece looks like a pendant, but such an interpretation would not explain the wear pattern just described.

IX. *Beads* (pl. 10r-v) – Bone beads are characteristic of the Zawi Chemi culture; in all sixty-five whole and fragmentary beads were recovered. The bone beads may be divided into a number of sub-types. Sub-type A is represented by forty-one examples, and is the most common one. These are tubular beads, usually made from hollow bird bones, but with some made out of mammal bones (pl. 10s). They range in size from 1.2x0.4 cm. to 3.3x0.8 cm. Sub-type B (seven examples) are flat, rectangular shaped beads (pl. 10t), which may in actuality be a variety of sub-type A. These beads range in size from 1.6x0.7 cm. to 1.8x0.9 cm., and are 0.4 cm. thick. Sub-type C (eleven examples) are large beads, barrel shaped or flat and broad (pl. 10r,u), perhaps divisible into two varieties. The barrel shaped ones, which are also more rounded, have large circular holes and thin walls. The broad flat beads have large, elliptical shaped holes. The more barrel shaped ones range in size from 1.4xca. 1.1 cm. to 1.9x1.2 cm., and the broad flat ones seem to average around 1.8x1.6 cm. The beads in this sub-type are usually well made and nicely finished.

Finally there is an interesting specimen (pl. 10v) which seems to represent beads in the process of manufacture. This is an elongate bone piece (3.5 cm. long), triangular in section. It has the characteristic beveled ends, but also has two V-shaped notches cut on its convex surface. The flat surface was purposely flattened. It seems likely that the notches represent the cutting guide lines for beads, and that three beads were to be made out of this piece.

Many of the beads, especially those in sub-type A, are made out of hollow bird bone, but mammal bone was also used for them. The beads appear to have been cut in a slanting plane, giving them beveled ends. Sometimes the ends are smoothed but left beveled, and sometimes the bevel was eliminated in the finished process. The beads are usually polished.

X. *Decorated bone pieces* (pl. 10w-ee) – The Zawi Chemi people sometimes decorated their bone objects with simple designs. There are thirty-seven bone pieces with some sort of decoration. Many are fragments so small that it is not possible to determine their tool type, let alone the over-all design. The bones may have carved, notched, incised, or perforated designs.

The carved bone pieces (pl. 10w,x) are small end pieces which have been carved to form a diamond shape, in fact they resemble a snake head (seen from above). One of them even has two small depressions, resembling eyes, making the snake head suggestion even more likely. Then there are two carved disc pieces, of unknown use. One is very thin, reportedly a piece of plasteron from a turtle carapace and rubbed smooth on both faces. The other is ovate in shape (3.5x2.6x0.9 cm.) hacked off at one end, with obvious cut marks at that end. It is not known if this piece was the desired end product or was discarded after the cutting.

There are nine notched pieces (pl. 10y,z), with cut notches along the sides. Characteristically they are on flat, polished bone pieces, some quite narrow (0.6 cm.), but they probably also occur on pieces more than 1.5 cm. wide. The notches are cut along the sides, usually alternating, but in one example they are opposite

There are sixteen bone pieces with incised decorations (pl. 10m,n,q,aa-dd), five of these also have perforations. The designs may be simple lineal ones such as variously spaced, variously sized parallel lines; curved and concentric; or arranged into simple geometric patterns. More complicated patterns such as crosshatchings or possibly herringbones are present, and the designs may be zoned. Only one piece suggests a naturalistic representation, but it is too fragmentary for sure identification. This one is of special note though for it resembles a carved slate piece from the Zawi Chemi occupation of Shanidar Cave.

There are about nine bone pieces in which there is one or a series of perforations, apparently not primarily for suspension (pl. 10k,l,bb,cc,ee). Some of the pieces are so fragmentary it is not possible to determine the number of holes in the original pattern. One piece has three holes in a row along the edge. The holes are along the edge or in a row diagonally across the width, and occur primarily on the tools with polished, non piercing ends and the flat, pointed tools. One specimen has an incomplete perforation; it is the butt end fragment of a narrow, polished tool, with a semi-circular notch, really an incomplete hole drilled through on one side.

There is a lot of miscellaneous used or worked bone pieces that have been grouped together as a convenience for description. Here are such things as articulation heads, usually with beveled ends, cut from their shafts during the manufacturing process. Interestingly enough, Dexter Perkins has identified one of these as from *Canus lupis* and one from *Ursus arctos*. There are also two unfused articulation heads which have been perforated, apparently for suspension; one has been identified as a *Cervus elaphus* metapodial. Then there are a number of blunt ends of broken tools, not classifiable because the working ends are missing. They vary from completely fashioned ends to unmodified articulation heads, some of them are perforated. There are more than a hundred shaft fragments too small to identify. A collection of cut bones, not yet formed into finished objects, is also present; most are flat rectangular pieces with beveled ends. Then there are bones with cut marks, apparently from the butchering process, and bones with what appear to be chewing marks on them.

5.5.2. Antler and Horn Industry

Several pieces of worked antler (red deer) and horn (sheep and/or goat) have been recovered from Zawi Chemi Shanidar. There is the tip end of a piece of antler, 10.7 cm. long and 2.0 cm. wide, which has been polished from about two to three cm. from the end through use (pl. 11d). On the concave face of this piece a large flake has been removed just below the tip. There is a second polished tip end, again with a largish flake removed from one face (pl. 11e). A third badly eroded specimen seems to resemble these two. Then there are two beveled pieces; one with a slight bevel at the tip end through use wear and one so beveled on both faces that it ends in a broad but sharp angled point (pl. 11f). This last piece measures 9.8 cm. in length and 3.2 cm. in width at the base.

There is the end fragment of a largish object, 3.1 cm. wide and 1.5 cm. thick, made from an *Ovis orientalis* horn core (pl. 11g) The object was worked so that the end is ogival shaped, but is thinned to a sharp edge in side view. The cross-section of the shaft is lenticular shaped.

There are at least four other pieces of horn or antler which seem to have been used. They had scratch or cut marks, or evidence of polishing.

5.5.3. Ivory Industry

There are two perforated mammal teeth, identified as probably *Cervus elaphus* (the red deer), which probably served as beads (pl. 11h). There are also two more such teeth in the collection, identical in appearance to the above, but unperforated.

5.5.4. Summary of the Zawi Chemi Bone, Antler, Horn, and Ivory Industries

In summarizing the bone, antler, horn, and ivory industries at Zawi Chemi Shanidar, we may make the following observations. Bone tools were characteristic of the Zawi Chemi culture and were probably used in such manufacturing processes as skin dressing, leather working, and some sort of matting, basketry, or netting. The awls (pl. 10a-e), of course, were used for piercing of some sort, most likely of leather and skin. From ethnographic data we know that awls were also used in basketry, especially in coiled basketry, to separate the coils during the sewing (Mason, 1904, pp. 245-246, 433, and fig. 40). Bone awls were also used in the making of the fiber strips used in basketry.

The flat pointed tools (pl. 10k-m) also suggest matting, weaving, or netting tools. Crowfoot (1957, fig. 273G) illustrates a similar bone tool from Ghassul (ca. 3000 B.C.) which he calls a "needle shuttle." This piece has a hole at the non-working end of the shaft similar to the one from Shanidar Cave illustrated in pl. 11a. The Zawi Chemi specimens could have one or more perforations somewhere on the shaft. Skinner (1921, pp. 307-308, fig. 21) illustrates two bone matting needles from the Menomini Indians of Wisconsin which resemble the Zawi Chemi tools. They are flat pieces, circa one foot long and half a foot wide, with one pointed and one blunt end, made out of buffalo or cow rib, with a single perforation in the center. They were used to sew together the flags of cattail for roofing mats. The Menomini also make somewhat similar shaped snowshoe needles out of bone (Skinner, 1921, p. 307, fig. 52). These are flat, double pointed needles, four to six inches long, and perforated in the middle. They are used in netting the babiche on snowshoes.

The tools from Zawi Chemi Shanidar with the non-piercing, polished ends, as already noted, are variable in size and shape, and were probably used for a variety of tasks. The heavier ones with the broader ends could have been used in skin working, possibly as fat scrapers (from the inside or non-hair surface of the skin). Somewhat similar tools are called skin dressing tools in the ethnographic literature (Mason, 1889, pl. LXIX, fig. 1; Wissler, 1910, fig. 34; Skinner, 1911, figs. 15a, 42). The more delicate tools in this type may have been basketry or matting tools of some sort.

The tiny points most probably were used in some sort of composite object—possibly a comb. The beads, of course, were for ornamentation and possibly the winged object shown in pl. 10q was a pendant. The Zawi Chemi people apparently liked to decorate their bone tools with simple designs.

The horn and antler tools may have been used in the chipped stone industry as flakers.

5.6. Architecture

A portion of a circular stone structure was exposed during the excavation of Test 1, and the entire feature, called Structure I (pl. 3a,b, and figs. 7-9), was exposed by the excavation of Cut 1. Architecture was absent in Cut 2 and in Test 2, so presently our knowledge of Zawi Chemi architecture is based on this single occurrence.

Structure I (pl. 3a,b, and figs. 7-9) is roughly circular in outline, and apparently had been rebuilt three times, the two rebuildings placed somewhat to the west of the earliest building. The circular enclosures measure roughly two meters in diameter, possibly with an entryway in the western section. The walls are composed of both small and large rocks; and a good number of fragmentary and sometimes complete tools (e.g., spall cores, querns, mullers, hammerstones, spall tools, etc.) are incorporated into the walls. No mortar is evident in the walls today. Such mortarless stone construction is still used in the area for field walls and simple animal shelters (pl. 3c).

The earliest structure (pl. 3b, and fig. 9) is the best preserved, and measures ca. 2.20 meters in diameter. Much of the wall is composed of small pieces of quartzite and limestone, but in one section at least larger blocks were used. The highest remaining section of wall is 36 cm. high and is composed of a big rock placed on smaller rocks. Apparently associated with this lowest construction are five shaped slabs, type XII in the Inventory of Pecked, Ground, or Polished Stone tools (Table 3, and pl. 6p). Three are lying flat, cracked in place outside the walls; one is standing on end outside the walls; and one is just inside the walls, perhaps fallen in (fig. 9). Some three meters south of this structure is the mass of goat/sheep skulls and wing bones from large birds, (primarily predators) associated with a reddened earth zone, and suggesting some sort of ritual, as described immediately below. The proximity of these items of probable ceremonial significance, leads to the supposition that Structure I may have served some special function.

Structure I seems to have been rebuilt twice, each somewhat to the west of the original building (pl. 3a, and figs. 7,8). These are more poorly preserved than the earliest construction, but appear to be oriented and constructed in much the same manner. To the east of these upper structures is an area of rock concentration (including many quern, muller, and spall tool pieces) mixed in with cultural refuse and much charcoal (fig. 8).

5.7. Mass of Animal Bones–Ritual (?) Paraphernalia

A mass of animal bones with patches of reddened earth is located just south of Structure I, in the 1.25-1.50 m. level of Cut 1 (pl. 12). The area of exposed bone concentration is 90x100 cm., but it seems likely that it continued beyond the limits of the excavation. Detailed studies of these bones and their cultural significance have been published elsewhere (R.L. Solecki, 1977), and need only be summarized here. The bones include the skulls of at least fifteen sheep and/or goats, most likely wild, and the bones (ninety percent of them are wing bones) from a minimum of seventeen birds, including four bearded vultures, one griffon vulture, seven white-tailed sea eagles, four small eagles, and one great bustard. All of these birds are from large-sized species, and all but the great bustard are raptorial birds. So we are dealing here with a very specialized collection consisting of wild goat and/or sheep skulls and the wing bones from predominantly large, predatory birds. These are certainly not the remains from an ordinary meal or even a feast, and probably represent some sort of ritual paraphernalia. The animal remains present here also surely are the results of the concerted hunting efforts of a goodly number of people—perhaps the entire village was involved.

We know from ethnographic and archaeological data that man has long endowed special powers to these great raptorial birds. Also rams' horns have been found in shrines at other prehistoric Near Eastern sites, e.g., Ganj Dareh and Çatal Hüyük. The bird wings in the Zawi Chemi collection seem to have been still in articulation when discarded, and thus we conclude that they were saved for their feathers to be used in such objects as feather fans, or that the wings themselves were used as part of a costume in a ritual. Just such a ritual scene, i.e., a human figure dressed in a vulture costume partaking in what seems to be a burial rite, is depicted in one of the murals from Çatal Hüyük in Shrine VII.21 (Mellaart, 1967, pl. 47, figs. 14,15). Interestingly enough, at Çatal Hüyük, bulls' heads and rams' heads are found in the same shrines with the vulture murals. This suggests that the goat/sheep skulls found with the wing bones at Zawi Chemi may be part of the same symbolism, paraphernalia for the same ritual.

CHAPTER 6

ENVIRONMENTAL BACKGROUND – POST PLEISTOCENE

Studies of late Pleistocene and early Recent vegetational patterns in the Near East have expanded considerably in the last decade or so, concentrating especially on two important problems: 1. the kind and degree of climate changes which accompanied the end of the Pleistocene and the beginning of the Recent ages in the region and 2. the development by man of domesticated plants from the wild cereals, legumes, etc., which were part of the native flora. Such palaeo-botanical studies are particularly important, for it is during the period we are concerned with in this paper that man began to exhibit ever greater control of his food supply through the cultivation of plants and the keeping of animals. We now have plant studies from a number of early village sites (e.g., Nahal Oren, Mureybit, Ali Kosh, Jarmo, Çayönü, Aceramic Hacilar, Beidha, Pre-Pottery Neolithic Jericho, Ramad), but as Van Zeist (1976, pp. 28-29) has pointed out it is not yet possible to present a general, overall picture for the development of agriculture in the Near East because of such problems as: the scattered nature of the site samples available; the uneven quality of the data; the problems in the exact dating of the sites, etc. Even so, huge strides have been made in recent years in our understanding the development of agriculture in the ancient Near East.

Climate studies based on pollen diagrams have also broadened greatly in recent years. So much so that in 1976 (Van Zeist, p. 38) was able to write:

> "The available palynological evidence has already forced us to a radical change in our thinking concerning a possible impetus for the beginning of food production. The palynological results have demonstrated convincingly that in the Near East there can be no question of a desiccation after the last glacial period. On the contrary, the humidity increased markedly in the period preceeding [sic] the introduction of agriculture and stock-breeding. The beginning of food production cannot have been induced by a reduction of the area which was suitable for a food collecting economy."

As of 1975, Van Zeist, Woldring, and Stapert (fig. 1) noted that pollen diagrams were now available for the following sites in the Near East: Mirabad and Zeribar (Iran); Bozova, Gölbaşi, Surmene-Agaçbaşi, Yeniçaga, Abant, Karamik Batakliği, Hoyran, Köyceğiz, Söğüt, Beyşehir (Turkey); Ghab, Sahl-Aâdra (Syria); and Huleh, Kinneret (Israel).

Lake Zeribar, located today in the Iranian Zagrosian Oak Forest zone, at an elevation of ca. 1300 meters, has produced sediment cores which provide climatological data on the late Quaternary and early Recent periods (Van Zeist and Wright, 1963, Van Zeist, 1967). In this particular area from ca. 14,000 B.P. onwards, the evidence shows that although changes occurred slowly, the annual precipitation as well as the temperature increased. Perhaps it was not until shortly before

10,000 B.P. that trees made their appearance in the Lake Zeribar region. From ca. 10,000 to 6000 B.P. there was a gradual increase in the tree pollen. Van Zeist (1969, p. 43) noted that for the period between ca. 10,000 and 8000 B.P. in western Iran the pollen record indicates that steppe forests were found in areas where nowadays the Zagrosian Oak Forest constitutes the natural vegetation. This implies that the vegetation in the Zagros mountains then had a drier character than today.

Mme. Leroi-Gourhan (1976) has analyzed the pollen sample from the site of Zarzi, a cave site at approximately the same elevation as Zawi Chemi Shanidar, and located some 140 kms. to the southeast in the Zagros. The main occupation at the site of Zarzi refers to the Zarzian (dated at ca. 12,000 years ago), in the same cultural tradition as Layer B2 of Shanidar Cave. Mme. Leroi-Gourhan noted that the flora at the Zarzi site was that of a steppe, very dry and without any doubt very cold, almost without trees. Liguliflorae Compositae were dominant and Cerealia-type pollens were extremely rare. She believes that it represented the end of the steppe period (ca. 14,000 B.P.), already described for Lake Zeribar.

At a somewhat later period, i.e., between 10,000 and 8000 B.P. the vegetation, in general in the Near East, would still have been more open than later in the Post-glacial when trees spread from their refuge areas. Van Zeist (1969, p. 43) made an interesting suggestion about the possibility that Rowanduz could have been just such a refuge area, and that tree growth could have continued here in the dry and cold period prior to 14,000 B.P. and later. He based this on the recorded modern mean annual precipitation of ca. 1000 mm. at stations in the Rowanduz area (elevation at about 1000 m. above sea level). Rowanduz it should be noted is located only some 35 kms. southeast (as the crow flies) of Zawi Chemi Shanidar, on the Rowanduz river, a branch of the Greater Zab. It should be further noted, however, that Rowanduz is at a higher elevation than Zawi Chemi Shanidar; the latter site being only ca. 425 meters in elevation, although it is surrounded by high mountains. Even so indications from the site of Zawi Chemi Shanidar, e.g., the presence of axes, adzes, gouges, and notched and denticulate tools suggests the presence of trees and a woodworking industry. Van Zeist makes one further interesting reference to late Quaternary refuge areas. He states (1969, p. 45) "If forest or steppe forest could survive in the Ruwandiz area, one may assume that cereals also found a refuge there. . .Like the trees, wild cereals would have spread from their refuge areas after 14,000 B.P."

Recently, important pollen evidence has been published for southwestern Turkey, at the opposite end of the arc of the greater Near East (Van Zeist, Woldring, and Stapert, 1975). This is an area which has much variation in topography and climate, a condition reflected in a very diversified and complex natural plant cover. The pollen evidence from the Söğüt and Karamik areas of southwestern Turkey suggests that in the period between 20,000 B.P. or older and ca. 14,000 B.P. steppe vegetation played an important role; today in both areas forests constitute the prevailing vegetation (ibid., p. 38 ff.). This evidence corroborates the predominantly steppe vegetation suggested by other diagrams for the eastern Mediterranean; and in the Lake Zeribar area in western Iran trees were completely absent from ca. 22,000 to 14,000 B.P. (ibid., 138). The scarcity of trees during full glacial times in the eastern Mediterranean area is primarily ascribed to a dry climate. It was much colder, of course, than the present, but cold would become a limiting factor for tree growth only at higher elevations (ibid., 139). Van Zeist, Woldring, and Stapert (ibid.) suggest that the coastal areas which at present receive much precipitation (1000 mm. and more) supported forest vegetations in full glacial times.

Van Zeist et. al. (1975) report a complicated mosaic of vegetational-climate zones for the late Pleistocene period in the eastern Mediterranean. From the pollen diagrams of the Karamik and Sogut areas in southwestern Turkey conditions became more favorable for tree growth after ca. 14,000 B.P., while diagrams from east-central Greece and northwest Syria indicate that at lower elevations, conditions for tree growth became extremely adverse in late glacial times, most probably as a result of a further increase in dryness. Between 12,000 and 11,500 B.P. conditions again became unfavorable for tree growth in the Karamik and Söğüt areas; they suggest (1975, p. 139) that the increase in dryness was the result of a further rise in temperature. Although there may have been minor expansions of trees after ca. 10,000 B.P., in the beginning of the post-glacial, steppe vegetations must still have prevailed in the greater part of southwestern Turkey. Forest vegetation expanded more considerably after ca. 8500 B.P. when we see a transition from steppe and forest-steppe to forests; but evidence suggests that there was not a uniform, synchronous transition in the vegetational patterns in the mountainous regions of southwestern Turkey. The Karamik and Söğüt diagrams suggest that at about 6000 B.P. humidity had approximately reached modern levels, although minor changes in humidity are noted for later periods as well. The conclusions that the immediate post-Pleistocene period was drier than the present day are similar to those already outlined for Lake Zeribar, and hold true for other parts of the eastern Mediterranean and the western Iranian Zagros zone. In all these areas the pollen diagrams suggest that modern conditions do not prevail until ca. 6500 or 6000 B.P. One further note should be made about the greater dryness of the immediate post-Pleistocene period as described by Van Zeist, Woldring, and Stapert (1975, p. 140):

> "Thus, the palynological evidence from various areas in the Eastern Mediterranean indicates that in early Postglacial times the climate was drier than at present. As has already been suggested elsewhere (Van Zeist 1969), this 'greater dryness' may not necessarily imply less precipitation. It is feasible that, as a result of higher temperatures or of a longer rainless period, the summers were drier. A greater summer dryness would have affected tree growth in particular."

Mme. Arlette Leroi-Gourhan has studied the pollen samples from Zawi Chemi Shanidar (1969 and Appendix III) and also has analyzed earlier and coeval pollen samples from Shanidar Cave (1969). Her conclusions on the Zawi Chemi Shanidar samples may be summarized here, but for a full discussion Appendix III should be consulted. Note should be made, as Mme. Leroi-Gourhan has pointed out, that since the Zawi Chemi pollen samples come from a village site, they are not to be considered natural samples but from an environment that has been disturbed by man to make his settlement. Furthermore, if the area around the village had been used for pasturage, even for a short time of the year, this would have affected the herbaceous vegetation, as the animals would eat off their favored foods even before flowering. Taking the above factors into account, she observed that the floral assemblage from Zawi Chemi, on the basis of palynological studies, suggested a steppe savanna with very few trees (never reaching 3% of the pollen sample during the Zawi Chemi period). She noted, furthermore, that although the tree pollen scarcely changed, the herbaceous flora could be differentiated into three phases, designated mainly by by changes in the Chenopodiaceae curve. At the base of the excavation the Chenopodiaceae were rare, increasing at about the 2.21 m. level until about the 1.90 m. level when they declined. The part of the sequence from 1.90 m. to .90 m. i.e., equivalent to the early portion and to much of the main Zawi Chemi occupation, saw a reduction of the Chenopodiaceae, and a scene in which the Liguliflorae Compositae predominated. This suggested to her a moister period than earlier when the Chenopodiaceae predominated.

Mme. Leroi-Gourhan also noted (Appendix III, and fig. 17) that above the 2.20 m. level there was a definite increase in the Gramineae pollen, Cerealia-type. She noted that it is not now possible to differentiate the wild Gramineae pollen ancestral to our cereals from those of their cultivated descendants. However, she believes that the discovery of an increase in the Cerealia-type pollens in a pollen diagram could be ascribed to two possible causes: a change in the climate or a change to agricultural techniques. She concludes that although some climate changes are reflected in the Zawi Chemi pollen diagram they are minor ones, and feels it is difficult to impart to them the necessary significance to have caused the increases in the Cerealia-type pollens as shown in fig. 17. She further notes that in the Proto-Neolithic level from Shanidar Cave she finds the Cerealia-type pollens also take on an important role. So the evidence suggests that during the Proto-Neolithic period important agricultural changes were taking place in Shanidar valley (and of course elsewhere). Cultural remains from Zawi Chemi Shanidar, e.g., the querns, mullers, pestles, mortar, etc. reinforce the view that the Zawi Chemi people were using large amounts of plant food in their diet. Unfortunately, we have as yet no plant remains from Zawi Chemi for the palaeo-botanists to study.

We can now summarize our knowledge of the vegetational pattern around the village site of Zawi Chemi, at ca. 8500 B.C., and indicate the sort of climate that is reflected from this pattern. Today the site is included in the Temperate to Hardy Forest Vegetation zone of the eastern Mediterranean region (Van Zeist, 1969, fig. 1). Van Zeist (ibid., p. 36) noted that forest vegetations can be subdivided into two major ecologic groups; and the area under consideration may be referred to as a Xeric forest type in which there is a more or less severe dry period in the summer. He (Van Zeist, ibid., p. 38) further noted that a few regional variations of this forest type exist, one being the Zagros Mountains of western Iran and north-eastern Iraq where the deciduous Persian oak (Quercus persica) is the most common tree. We know from pollen studies in various parts of the Near East, that although it was gradually getting wetter and warmer in the 9th millennium B.C., and trees, cereals, and other plants were spreading out from refuge areas, today areas which have forest vegetations (or would have if not vandalized by man) in the early Holocene were still characterized by a steppe-forest or steppe-savanna vegetation.

At the village site of Zawi Chemi, Mme. Leroi-Gourhan has found that a steppe-savanna type of vegetation was characteristic. However, note must be made of the fact that this sample was from a village site, and has been skewed by the activities of man. The sample was probably further affected by the activities of husbanded sheep, which seem to have been kept by the later inhabitants of the Proto-Neolithic Zawi Chemi village. They, of course, would have eaten away at any favored food that grew around the village. The low percentage of aboreal pollen (never reaching 3%) must in part be due to man's activities in clearing the site for his village and perhaps also for his fields. We find such tools as: axes, adzes, chisels, denticulates, notches, etc. at the site, presumably to fell trees and to shape the wood from them into various useful items.

At about the time of the initial occupation of Zawi Chemi Shanidar, the Liguliflorae Compositae begin to increase in popularity until they dominate the scene (fig. 17), indicating to Mme. Leroi-Gourhan a moister period than earlier. At the same time there is a noticeable increase in the Cerealia-type pollen. Although Cerealia-type pollens can be found in both cultivated and wild cereal species as well as in other wild grasses in the Near East, and they cannot presently be distinguished from one another, the noticeable increase in Cerealia-type pollen does indicate either a change in climate or a change in agricultural technique. Although conditions were getting better (i.e., warmer and wetter) for the spread of the cereals at this time, Mme. Leroi-Gourhan does not believe that the change was of significant enough a nature to cause the increase noted in the Zawi Chemi pollen diagram (fig. 17). We are, therefore, left with the alternate hypothesis that the people of Zawi Chemi were practicing some sort of agricultural activity. This conclusion is reinforced by the presence at the site of various food processing tools in good numbers.

I should just like to say one final word on the subject of the proposed Rowanduz Refuge area for trees and cereal plants suggested by Van Zeist (1969, p. 43), an area located only some 35 kms. southeast of Shanidar. Shanidar valley could, theoretically, have received these important floral species early in the Holocene as climate warmed and rainfall increased, and the inhabitants of Shanidar valley could at an early date have taken advantage of the ever more abundant plant foods to establish an early village.

CHAPTER 7

CONCLUSIONS

7.1. Summary of the Material Remains

Zawi Chemi material culture is characterized by the great variety of techniques utilized and the numbers of different tool types produced. Stone tools were made by chipping, flaking, pecking, and grinding, and there was also some limited use of stone polishing. Bone tools and objects, mainly undecorated but sometimes decorated with simple incised or carved designs, are also present. A few horn, antler, and ivory pieces are included in the inventory. There are ornaments in the form of beads and pendants made of various materials, and along with the simple decorated pieces mentioned above, represent some of the earliest occurrences of exotic items from the region. No ceramics or clay objects are associated with the Proto-Neolithic occupation at Zawi Chemi Shanidar.

The stone tools are divided into three broad industries: a. chipped, subdivided into microlithic (fig. 10) and standard sized (figs. 11-14) components; b. pecked, ground, or polished (pls. 4-8, and figs. 15,16a-g); and c. flaked (pl. 9, and fig. 16h,i). The chipped stone industry, summarized in Table 6, is characterized by the small number of tools (4.9%) in relation to simple used pieces (9.0%) and especially to the large numbers of knapping waste pieces (84.6%). The workmanship may be characterized as of modest quality, especially in comparison to the earlier, local Upper Palaeolithic (Baradostian) and Epi-Palaeolithic/Mesolithic (Zarzian) industries.

The microlithic component represents a minor (26.0%) but still important part of the total chipped stone inventory; within the microlithic component there is a strong element (61.1%) of backed blades (both plain and with retouched ends) and a geometric element represented primarily by lunates (20.2%).

The standard sized tools (74.0% of the total chipped stone tool inventory) are divided into eleven broad types plus a miscellaneous category and one composed of broken tools. Two types, however, predominate in the assemblage. These include the denticulates and the related notched pieces, which together comprise 35.6%, and the pièces esquillées 30.8%. Scrapers of various kinds comprise slightly less than 15.0%, and distinctive, well made borers ca. 3.0%. Backed blades are only a minor component, and only two blades with weak sickle sheen are present. Burins are also a minor element, making up less than 0.6%.

The associated cores (pl. 13) are characteristically made from river pebbles and are quite variable in color and texture. Most are worked down to small size, some to exhausted nubbins. None of the cores recovered are of sufficient size, in their present form, to have produced the

TABLE 6

Summary of Chipped Stone Industry From Cut 2

Type	Numbers	Percent of Tools	Overall Percent
Total Tools	2,119		4.9
Microlithic Sized	550	26.0	
Standard Sized	1,569	74.0	
Cores	682*		1.5
Used Pieces	3,894		9.0
Debris	36,482*		84.6

*Figures approximated by doubling the numbers in the half of the Cut 2 collections in the U.S.A. available for study.

flakes and blades used for the majority of the standard sized tools. Several types of cores are outlined, with single platform pebble cores the most common, followed in popularity by two platform and three platform cores, with other minor types present. The cores represent ca. 1.5% of the total chipped stone inventory.

Used pieces, flakes, blades, and trimming pieces, account for about 9.0% of the total chipped stone inventory. Both microlithic and standard sized used pieces are present; in the former group blades are more common and in the latter, flakes appear to have been used about three times more often than blades. These pieces show little to heavy evidence of use.

Flint knapping debris represents the overwhelming amount (84.6%) of all chipped stone material from Zawi Chemi; in comparison to only 4.9% for all tools; 1.5% for cores; and 9.0% for used pieces. This indicates that a great deal of flint knapping was done right there at the site, close to the main source of the raw materials, i.e., the river pebbles. It also suggests that a great deal of knapping was done to produce the few tools found. This may be a reflection of the poor quality of the raw material utilized or the modest technical skill of the knappers. Another possibility that suggests itself is that the tools may have been used and discarded at another site in the yearly cycle of the Zawi Chemi people; we have postulated elsewhere in this paper that the site of Zawi Chemi village may have been only seasonally occupied.

Zawi Chemi also contains an important pecked, ground, or polished stone element (Table 4). Except for very rare pieces utilizing such techniques which appear to have been associated with

Epi-Palaeolithic industries in the Near East, e.g., Zarzian at Zarzi (Garrod, 1930) and Kebaran at Ein Gev I (Bar Yosef, 1970, pp. 122, 170-171), such techniques were not characteristic of these or other earlier cultures. Zawi Chemi on the other hand, represents a period characterized by much experimentation with such techniques and the production of an impressive variety of associated tool types. The large numbers of such tools found at Zawi Chemi Shanidar, especially in comparison with roughly coeval sites, suggests either a production center at the site (because of the proximity of the raw materials) or the manufacture of new tools as the site was seasonally reoccupied. Many of these tools are too heavy to have been carried about on seasonal rounds, and consequently were left where they were made.

Some of these tools must have been associated with the preparation of plant food: e.g., the mullers (pl. 4a-d), querns (pl. 4e-i), mortars (pl. 4j), and probably also the pounders (pl. 5g) and shaped slabs (pl. 6p). Also found are hammerstones (pl. 5h-q), lighter pecking stones (pl. 6a-e, and fig. d-g), and abraders (pl. 5a-f, and fig. 15a-c), tools probably used for the new technologies as well as for traditional purposes. Stone rubbers (pl. 6f-m, and fig. 15h-j) were probably also tools for the manufacturing of other tools or objects; it has been suggested that the facetted rubbers may have been used to retouch chipped stone pieces (communication, R.S. Solecki).

Stone celts made their earliest appearance in the Zagros at this time, and continued to be important tools into much later periods. The Zawi Chemi celts (pl. 7, and fig. 16a-g) were very likely used as axes and adzes, and possibly also as gouges, chisels, and wedges. Usually the celts were flaked to shape and then polished bits were fashioned, although flaked bits may have been used also. A few examples of roughly allover smoothed/polished specimens are present. Celts are found almost exclusively in the middle and upper portions of the Zawi Chemi period deposits or in disturbed contexts (e.g., on the surface). This indicates that they were introduced into the site sometime after the initial settlement had been made. They must have been important for the clearing of forests and were possibly used for tilling the soil. Such tools were also used for working wood into a variety of useful tools and objects.

A certain number of exotic items or ornaments are found at Zawi Chemi village, again representing cultural innovations in this area. Grooved stones (pl. 6q-u) were made out of specially selected stones, chlorite or related materials. These occur in a variety of sub-types, some of which may have been straighteners for cane shafts, items possibly related to the spread of the bow and arrow at about this time. The raw materials selected for the grooved stones were too soft to have permitted their use as grinders or smoothers, without the addition of some sort of abrasive material.

Rare ornaments in the form of marble and other stone pendants (pl. 8a-j, and fig. 15k-m); marble, chlorite, and other stone beads (pl. 8k-m, and fig. 15n); such other exotics as marble and other stone discs (pl. 8o-q, and fig. 15o); and engraved and punctated stones (pl. 8r, and fig. 15p) are also present at Zawi Chemi. It should be noted that no stone bracelets or rings were recovered from the site.

A category of flaked stone tools (Table 5, pl 9, and fig. 16h,i) are also included in the Zawi Chemi inventory. These tools were made by removing medium to large sized flakes from a core, and then either the flakes or the cores were utilized as tools. Most common are the spall tools (pl. 9j-o); thin, broad flakes struck from around the edges of boulder cores, with naturally sharp, thin cutting edges. Some five hundred of these were recovered from the excavations at Cut 2 alone. Similar tools, on the basis of ethnographic data (Rainey, 1940, p. 301) are known to have been used for skin scraping. Use studies by R.S. Solecki suggest that these tools might have been used for chopping (tall grass was used in the experiment) on a wooden surface. Another characteristic flake tool type is the chopper (pl. 9a-i) which occurs in a number of sub-types. The working edges of the choppers are either unifacially or bifacially produced. Light and heavy duty chisels (pl. 9s,t, and fig. 16h,i) are also present, as are some crude flaked specimens which may have been used.

In addition to the worked stone pieces described above, the Zawi Chemi people also collected and kept a number of odd items: e.g., lumps of lustrous taconite (pl. 8s,t), pieces of yellow and red ochre, fossil invertebrates (pl. 8u,v), pieces of stalagmite/stalagtite, a small quartz crystal, and bits of various minerals.

Bone tools and ornaments (pls. 10,11b,c) are also charactertistic of the Zawi Chemi culture, and again represent an important new industry in the area. Piercing tools with sharp pointed ends in a number of styles are most common, but tools with rounded, flat pointed, or beveled ends are also known. A single haft (pl. 11b,c) for the insertion of microliths, possibly a sickle haft, was also recovered. Tiny bone points are present and bone ornaments in the form of a variety of beads and a single pendant are all present. A small number of the bone pieces are decorated with simple incised lineal or carved designs; this represents, on the basis of present knowledge, some of the earliest art work in the region. Minor antler, horn, and ivory industries (pl. 11d-h) are also present at Zawi Chemi Shanidar.

7.2. Comparisons With Other Sites

A Zawi Chemi occupation is found in Shanidar Cave (R.S. Solecki, 1955, 1963), located some four kilometers away in the Baradost mountains. This occupation, Layer B1, dated at 10,600±300 years ago (Solecki and Rubin, 1958) is above the Zarzi layer, Layer B2, and below Layer A, dated from the Neolithic to the present. A number of Zawi Chemi period burials were recovered from Shanidar Cave; in a cemetery area in the rear of the cave (Ferembach, 1970) and an isolated one in the front of the cave. Grave goods were found with a number of these burials. Stone pavements and stone clusters also are associated.

Within the Zagros, Zawi Chemi also has close cultural parallels with the site of Karim Shahir, and shows resemblances to the sites of M'lefaat and Gird Chai on the basis of preliminary reports (Braidwood and Howe, 1960); viewing of some of the material finds from these sites by the present author; and correspondences and discussions with the field investigators,

B. Howe, R. Braidwood, and L. Braidwood[4]. Close parallels could be noted especially between Zawi Chemi and Karim Shahir, the latter site located some 150 kms. to the southeast. Although a broad scatter of stones at the site of Karim Shahir is reminiscent of Zawi Chemi, no definite structures were outlined there.

The Karim Shahir excavations exposed some five hundred and fifty square meters (B. Howe, letter, Jan. 17, 1978), a little more than double that so far exposed at Zawi Chemi (in total ca. 250 square meters). The depth of the excavations at Karim Shahir ranged from a few centimeters to nearly four meters (in one restricted area), but the occupation was represented by only a thin layer near the surface. Even so the site was rich in cultural remains, more than 70,000 chipped stone pieces were recovered, including tools, used pieces, cores, and trimming debris (B. Howe, letter, Jan. 17, 1978).

The chipped tool inventories of the two sites exhibited many similarities, although important differences are evident as well. First, there is a larger proportion of flint knapping debris at Zawi Chemi, perhaps a reflection of the proximity of the raw materials. Both contain a microlithic component, but purposely retouched microlithic sized tool types seem to be more abundant at Zawi Chemi; and of special note is the absence, in significant numbers of such geometric microliths as lunates at Karim Shahir and their presence at Zawi Chemi. In both industries notched and denticulated pieces are characteristic, but at Karim Shahir they are about twice as common. There are no pièces esquillées at Karim Shahir. Interestingly enough, when these tools which are found in large numbers at Zawi Chemi, are added to the denticulate-notched group of tools, the total approximates the Karim Shahir notched-denticulate figures. It has been suggested that all these tools were used for wood working. End scrapers and side scrapers resemble each other at the two sites, as do the double backed borers. At both sites, blades and flakes with sickle sheen are very rare, and obsidian virtually absent.

While the chipped stone industries are quite similar at the two sites (presumably reflecting common traditions and similar functional patterns), the remainder of the lithic industry exhibits a number of significant differences. These may represent seasonally restricted activities carried out at Zawi Chemi, or new cultural activities, or are perhaps the results of contacts between the Zawi Chemi people and groups outside the immediate area. Ground, pecked, or polished stone tools are very common at Zawi Chemi and relatively rare at Karim Shahir (especially considering the size of the exposure at the latter site). Querns, boulder mortars, mullers, and pestles are present only in small numbers at Karim Shahir. Hammer-stones are present at both sites, and one Zawi Chemi type, VIID-Greenstone, can be duplicated at Karim Shahir. Celts also are quite similar at the two sites, but again appear to be more abundant at Zawi Chemi. Grooved stones occur at both locations, but at Karim Shahir are limited to only one type, XIIIA. Pendants and beads are found at the two sites, but of different styles, and Karim Shahir has bracelet fragments, items not yet found at Zawi Chemi.

---

[4]The final report of Karim Shahir is in press, and the present author wishes to thank the investigators for permission to publish this summary here.

The common Zawi Chemi flakes stone industry, especially the choppers and the spall tools, appears to be absent at Karim Shahir.

The bone industry at Karim Shahir is more limited in numbers of pieces and in variety of tool types; also no decorated pieces are reported from that site. On the other hand two lightly baked clay figures are present at Karim Shahir, and no worked clay objects have as yet turned up at Zawi Chemi.

Tell M'lefaat located along the banks of the Khazir, a branch of the Greater Zab, was tested by the Braidwood group (Braidwood and Howe, 1960, pp. 50-52). Here a pit house was excavated, and two well marked floors with stone concentrations were identified; all suggesting a settlement of long enough duration for architectural renovations to have been made. Some of the architectural activity reported from this site is reminiscent of that at Zawi Chemi. The chipped stone industry of Tell M'lefaat is said to be reminiscent of Karim Shahir and Gird Chai (Braidwood and Howe, 1960, p. 51). The site "yielded a fair proportion of usually fragmentary boulder mortars, pestles, querns and rubbing stones, as well as ground and polished celts." (Braidwood and Howe, 1960, p. 51). Braidwood and Howe (1960, p. 52) noted that the celts from M'lefaat are predominantly pecked, ground, and polished, unlike the Karim Shahir and Zawi Chemi ones which, for the most part, are chipped to shape with polished bits. In respect to celt typology, Zawi Chemi is more like Karim Shahir, but in quantity of ground stone objects, seemingly close to M'lefaat. We still can agree, however, with the Braidwood and Howe conclusion (1960, p. 52) "that the Zawi Chemi Shanidar assemblage fits into the general range of M'lefaat and Karim Shahir."

The site of Gird Chai (Braidwood and Howe, 1960, pp. 54-55) was located on a ridge overlooking the Greater Zab, down river from Zawi Chemi Shanidar. It was tested by the Braidwood group but not further excavated because of later period disturbances. The flint industry is reported to be close to that of Karim Shahir and M'lefaat. A ground, pecked, and polished stone industry is found on the surface of the site, but there is little "in situ" evidence, and the chipped celts recall those of Karim Shahir rather than M'lefaat (Braidwood and Howe, 1960, p. 55).

Outside the Zagros mountain area, we may turn to a study of the roughly coeval (in part at least) Natufian culture of the Palestine area for comparisons with Zawi Chemi. In a recent study Henry (1973, p. 7) summarized Natufian culture as follows:

> "The Natufian has traditionally been defined as exhibiting incipient architecture (stone pavements and circular stone walls), burials, worked bone (harpoons, awls, and gorgets), ground stone objects (querns, pestles, and bedrock mortars), ornamental objects (dentalia shells and bone pendants), art *mobilier* (calcite and bone figures), and a predominantly microlithic flint industry (Garrod, 1932). The flint industry is generally characterized by high frequencies of geometric microliths, pieces bearing sheen (sickle blades), and large massive pieces (scrapers, denticulates and notches)."

Henry noted that although Natufian assemblages show a general similarity in tool kit, variability does occur. He concluded (Henry, 1973, p. 20) that "it is probably that time, other cultures, and environmental pressures were all factors contributing to the observed artifactual variability among the Natufian assemblages."

Natufian sites, according to Henry (1973, p. 188) were primarily limited to the "hill zone and plateau areas of Palestine, except for Eynan and Jericho which are located in the Jordan Valley near springs at the very edge of the hill country," and that the placement of the settlements was determined by the distribution of wild barley and emmer wheat. The presence of abundant bedrock mortars, pestles, querns, and grinding stones, as well as many pieces with sickle sheen strongly suggest the processing of plant food at these sites. Henry (1973, p. 189) believes that, "It is also doubtful that the Natufians were actually cultivating cereals, for the Natufian settlement pattern seems to correspond to the natural habitat of the cereals, and therefore, obviates cultivation." He concluded (Henry, 1973, pp. 189-190) that although animals still provided the more important portion of the diet, the supplemental wild grain foods were very valuable to their subsistence pattern. This adaptive strategy, according to Henry (1973, p. 198) was "unique to the Natufian at this time (8000-10,000 B.C.) in Palestine," and that "The relatively secure subsistence base seems to have indirectly percipitated the appearance of rudimentary architecture and incipient village settlements in the Natufian."

Zawi Chemi village appears to be a reflection of the same adaptive forces that have been described for the Natufian. Zawi Chemi, although located in the Baradost mountains is at a relatively modest elevation, 425 meters, within the altitudional range of many of the Natufian sites. Archaeological evidence from both areas, the Levant and the Zagros, suggests that plant food was being utilized as part of the diet (even though direct evidence for domestication is lacking), but that there was still a heavy dependence of animal food sources. In the case of Zawi Chemi, as already described, we have evidence suggestive of the introduction of domesticated sheep late in the occupation. On the basis of a broad based subsistence pattern both cultures (Natufian and Zawi Chemi) were able to establish at least semi-permanent villages with simple architecture, and both witnessed, if not the introduction, at least the widespread acceptance of new stone working techniques and a whole host of new tool types. In addition a rich bone industry is characteristic of both the Natufian and Zawi Chemi, and exotics and decorated objects are present in both cultures. Similar Zawi Chemi and Natufian burial patterns with associated grave goods may also be noted. Apparently the same sort of cultural flowering and elaboration could be observed developing in the two areas at this time.

Even if the Natufian and Zawi Chemi may be considered as part of the same broad horizon, they each also belonged to different traditions and exhibit differences which tie them to their own local heritages (e.g., the use of ridge-backed retouch in the Natufian). Also some of the differences must reflect idiosyncratic solutions to similar cultural problems (e.g. blades with sickle sheen in the Natufian and possibly the spall tools in the Zawi Chemi). Other characteristics may reflect environmental differences; e.g., the presence of celts (both axes and adzes) suggests that Shanidar valley may have been more wooded at that time, an idea reinforced by the higher proportion of denticulates, notches, and perhaps also the pièces esquillées at Zawi Chemi. Chronology may be another factor to be reckoned with here; the two dates we have for Zawi Chemi are both ca. 8500 B.C., while the Natufian is believed to date from ca. 8000 to 10,000 B.C. (Henry, 1973, p. 192). In any event, we must look to such multifaceted explanations if we are to realize meaningful intercultural relationships.

7.3. Cultural and Ecological Overview

The site of Zawi Chemi Shanidar is located in Shanidar valley, a part of the rugged Zagros mountain chain in northern Iraq. Although surrounded by high mountains, the valley floor on which the site is located is only 425 meters in elevation. It is situated on the first prominent terrace on the left bank of the Greater Zab river, a branch of the Tigris. The site lies in a modern wheat field, adjacent to a permanent spring and the small Kurdish village of Shanidar. Field plowing has brought up artifacts from the Proto-Neolithic village of Zawi Chemi to the surface, which on the basis of surface collections extended over an area approximately 250x275 meters (almost 70,000 square meters). Only a small portion of the site has been excavated (during two field seasons, 1956-1957 and 1960); in all an area of 112 square meters was excavated in part to a depth of three meters.

Two distinct cultural occupations are present at the site of Zawi Chemi Shanidar, corresponding to Layers A (Modern) and B (Proto-Neolithic). Layer A, the upper one, refers essentially to the first fifty centimeters of deposit although pits dug into lower strata are associated. Layer A on the basis of cultural materials has been dated at no earlier than the 6th century A.D. The lower layer, Layer B, below fifty centimeters to native soil refers to the Proto-Neolithic, Zawi Chemi occupation, dating from ca. 10,870±300 years ago (Solecki and Rubin, 1958, p. 1446). A similar occupation (Layer B1) is present in nearby Shanidar cave, and dates from approximately the same period, ca. 10,600±300 years ago (Solecki and Rubin, 1958, p.1446).

Zawi Chemi may be viewed as culturally transitional between the Epi-Palaeolithic Zarzian and the later, fully settled villages of the region (e.g. Ganj Dareh, Jarmo, etc.). A chipped stone industry with cultural ties to the earlier Epi-Palaeolithic is present, with many of the earlier types still used, and still with a strong microlithic element (including geometrics in the form of lunates), but with workmanship of only modest quality and with an enormous amount of flint knapping debris and simple used pieces in relation to purposely manufactured tools.

If the chipped stone industry gives one the impression of the end of a long tradition, certainly the rest of the material culture impresses one in just the opposite direction. In fact what most characterizes Zawi Chemi culture is the richness and variety of the other tools, and the many technological and even artistic innovations characteristic of it. It is a period of great experimentation, which makes it particularly interesting to the study of human cultural evolution. The pecked and ground stone tools occur in great numbers and varieties, and except for odd pieces seemingly associated with earlier assemblages, all are innovations of the Proto-Neolithic period in southwestern Asia. It also marks the introduction of stone polishing techniques for the production of more efficient and durable cutting edges. These are new technologies for new ways of living. The flaked tools also represent in a sense innovations, for although such tools are characteristic of the earliest human cultures (e.g. Lower Palaeolithic) for some reason this flake tool tradition diminished in importance during the Middle, Upper, and epi-Paleolithic periods, only to reappear again at this time. Such tools e.g., choppers, spall tools, are not characteristic of the Zagros Mousterian, Baradostian, or Zarzian, the known Palaeolithic cultures in the region.

The bone industry is greatly elaborated during the Zawi Chemi period, as it also is in the roughly coeval Natufian of the eastern Mediterranean. Well made bone tools in a variety of types are characteristic of Zawi Chemi, and some are decorated with simple incised or carved designs. This is the earliest art work in the Zagros region, and along with the bone, stone, and ivory beads, and bone and stone pendants indicate a growing elaboration and richness of culture not known previously in the region.

Zawi Chemi village was built in a favored location, rich in a variety of natural resources. Possibly simple flood plain agriculture was practised at the site, along the banks of the Greater Zab river (pl. 3d) The presence of so many tools for the preparation of plant food, as well as the palynological evidence suggests that the Zawi Chemi people were using plant food of some kind. The area was also rich in wild game, as evidenced by the large numbers of animal bones found at the site, and meat must have still formed a good portion of the diet. Dexter Perkins' studies (1964) of the Zawi Chemi faunal remains have shown that in the lower portion of the occupation Cervus elaphus (red deer) formed the major portion of the meat diet along with Ovis orientalis (sheep), but by the end of the Zawi Chemi occupation domestic sheep were present and were by far the dominant food animal. Capra hircus aegagrus (wild goat) was also hunted by the Zawi Chemi people. It should also be noted that snail shell (Helix salomonica) concentrations are found scattered throughout the occupation, and it is presumed that these creatures were also eaten by the inhabitants of the valley. Again the economic pattern suggests a period of innovation and experimentation, and one that provided the local inhabitants with a broadly based, stable food supply permitting the establishment of at least semi-permanent villages.

Trade in a few specialized items was going on in the Zagros at that time: e.g., the greenstone used for the sub-type VIId hammerstones and some of the chisels; the special stones favored for the celts; and chlorite used for the grooved objects. The widespread obsidian trade had not yet been opened up in the region, as evidenced by the virtual lack of this material at Zawi Chemi and Karim Shahir.

The ninth millenium B.C. was a time of some climate change in this part of the world, on the basis of vegetational studies from core samples and other evidence. Van Zeist (1976, p. 38) noted that recent palynological evidence shows that the period immediately after the last glaciation in southwestern Asia was not one of great dessication but that, on the contrary, one in which humidity increased markedly. This was the period just prior to the introduction of domesticated plants and animals in the area. The evidence further indicates that the post-Pleistocene climate continued to gradually get wetter and warmer until it reached modern levels about 6000 B.P.

Even during the cold and dry late Pleistocene period there must have been refuge areas where trees and also the wild cereals and other plants were able to survive. Van Zeist (1968, p. 43) suggests Rowanduz as just such a refuge area. Rowanduz is located only some thirty-five kilometers southeast from Zawi Chemi Shanidar, on the Rowanduz river, a branch of the Greater Zab. Shanidar valley because of its close proximity to this proposed refuge area and for other geographic reasons, probably was in a favored position to receive trees and plants as they spread out of a Rowanduz refuge area, as favorable post-Pleistocene climatic conditions developed.

Mme. Leroi-Gourhan's studies of the pollen from Zawi Chemi Shanidar (Appendix III) has provided us with a number of interesting findings. It should be pointed out that as these samples are from a village site, they do not constitute "natural samples" but represent an environment already disturbed by man and his animals. Even so we note her valuable conclusions as follows: The pollen evidence suggested a steppe-savanna environment with very few trees (never reach 0.3% of the sample) during the Zawi Chemi period. This conclusion may well be a reflection of the work of man, cutting down the trees to make his settlement. We know that the Zawi Chemi people had celts, and likely used them to fell trees as well as to fashion wooden objects. We also know that such wood working tools as denticulates and notched pieces made up an important element in their flint tool kit. Mme. Leroi-Gourhan noted further that although the tree pollen scarcely changed, there were changes in the herbaceous flora, suggesting that the early and most of the main Zawi Chemi occupation was a moister period. She also noted that during the Zawi Chemi occupation there was a definite increase in the gramineae pollen, Cerealia-type, which she ascribed to a change to agricultural techniques.

Zawi Chemi village, therefore, on the basis of present evidence, was occupied at a time (ninth millenium B.C.) when Shanidar valley was probably more open than today, with more steppe and fewer trees (the modern picture, of course, has been badly skewed by the activities of man and herded animals). Still the cultural material excavated from Zawi Chemi suggests that trees were felled to clear the land (for living areas or possibly for fields) and to provide raw materials for manufactures. The site was located in a favored position to receive the vegetational benefits of the increasing amelioration of climate in the post-Pleistocene period. Possibly its relatively low elevation at ca. 425 meters and its sheltered valley setting, as well as its permanent fresh water spring made it a particularly attractive area for early settlers. Furthermore, it was situated along the banks of the Greater Zab river which provided a valuable source of materials, in the form of pebbles and larger cobbles, for a variety of stone industries. Portions of the river banks were probably also covered with rich alluvial soil as they are today (pl. 3d). It should be noted that Shanidar valley lies within the zone of the wild prototypes of barley and wheat (Helbaek, 1959, p. 365, fig. 1). Although, as yet we have no actual plant remains from the site, on the basis of the cultural evidence (abundant querns, mullers, pounders, etc.) we infer that plant food was processed there. Shanidar valley was then rich in wild animal life, and the Zawi Chemi people still depended to a good measure on these creatures for food. Dr. Perkins (1964) has suggested on the basis of his studies that domesticated sheep were introduced into Zawi Chemi village, and by the end of the occupation became the dominant food animal.

As to the physical nature and areal extent of the Zawi Chemi village, we still have only limited information. On the basis of present knowledge we cannot be sure if the village was occupied year round or only seasonally. We tend to believe that the latter interpretation is the more likely one. Local Kurdish peoples still live in open villages during the warmer months and move into the shelter of the nearby Shanidar cave or other shelters during the winter season. On the basis of present information, we believe that the ninth millenium was even colder than the region is today, and it would seem logical for the inhabitants then to have found a sheltered spot to winter in. There is a Zawi Chemi occupation in nearby Shanidar cave, for which a roughly coeval date of 10,600±300 years has been obtained (Solecki and Rubin, 1958, p. 1446). Also the presence of heavy tools in such large numbers at the site of Zawi Chemi village, as well as the very small numbers of chipped tools in relation to the large amount of knapping debris found there, might be attributable to a pattern of transhumance.

The architectural picture of the village is still only poorly understood. Only one structure, rebuilt three times, has been excavated so far. It was stone walled, roughly circular in shape, averaging two meters in diameter. As a special, seemingly ritual deposit of goat skulls and bones, primarily wing bones from large predatory birds, was found just outside this structure, it may be that we are dealing with a ceremonial building of some kind (pls. 3a,b,12).

The people of Zawi Chemi, although they lived a simple life in a mountain fastness, showed evidence of growing cultural elaboration. What characterized the material remains found at the site more than anything else, was the great variety of the tools and the variety of the techniques that were used to manufacture them. The site represented a period of unusual experimentation and innovation in both material culture and lifeways. Zawi Chemi was not, of course, a unique cultural phenomenon; roughly coeval settled villages were also being established in other favored locations in southwestern Asia.

APPENDIX I

March 28, 1969

Dr. Rose Solecki
Department of Anthropology
Columbia University
New York, N.Y.

Dear Dr. Solecki:

Last evening at Dr. Porada's Seminar for Near Eastern Archaeology Dr. Solecki showed me the rubbing of the reverse of your coin, which I said I would be happy to try to identify. As corroborated by Joan Fagerlie, our curator of Roman coins, it is a bronze follis struck between ca. 498 and 538/9 A.D., at Constantinople during the reign of Anastasius I (491-518), Justin I (518-527), or Justinian I (527-565).

The large central M proclaims its value as a follis of 40 nummia. A cross appears above it, and a star to l. and r. CON in the exergue denotes the mint of Constantinople; while the epsilon beneath the M refers to the fifth officina or workshop at the mint, of which there were five (A through E).

Anastasius introduced this large bronze follis and its smaller denominations ca. 498. From 538/9 onward in Justinian's reign, the date of issue is recorded on the reverse, and a facing head of the emperor replaces the profile view. Hence your coin must have been struck between ca. 498 and 538/9. It might be possible to determine which emperor if parts of the legend on the obverse are still discernible:

DNANASTA SIVUSPPAVA (Anastasius), *cf., BMC* 28, p. 4;
DNIVSTI NVSPPAVC (Justin), *cf., BMC* 27, p. 14;
DNIVSTINI ANVSPPAVC (Justinian), *cf., BMC* 37, p. 30.

The BMC references are taken from the *Catalogue of the Imperial Byzantine Coins in the British Museum*, by W. Wroth, London, 1908.

Sincerely yours,

Nancy M. Waggoner (Mrs.)
Ass't Curator of Greek Coins
The American Numismatic Society

APPENDIX II

EVIDENCE OF METALLURGY AT ZAWI CHEMI SHANIDAR

Isabella M. Drew

Description of Samples Examined and Results of Tests Performed

BAKED CLAY GROUP

Box A (Sample 1 = 36/IV)

Small, irregular lumps of reddish-orange baked clay. Thin section of sample 36/IV, which appears typical of this group, showed fragments of quartzite and chert in a red-brown matrix of baked clay; the glassy, baked structure is beginning to devitrify around the edges of the fragment, and along crevasses. The X-ray diffractometer pattern exhibits weak quartz reflections.

Box B (Sample 2 = 87/IV) (pl. 14a)

Very similar to Box A in that it consists of a number of small, irregular lumps of baked clay. The thin section (87/IV) was very similar to 36/IV, except that there may be slightly more coarse fragments present in the baked clay matrix.

Box F (Sample 7 = 65/IV; Sample 8 = 87/IV)

Thin sections show structure very similar to samples in Box A (36/IV) and B (87/IV), except that tubular holes are present with gray residue at edges.

UNBAKED CLAY

Box D (Sample 3 = 87/IV) (pl. 14b)

Irregular lump of unbaked clay. Thin section shows quartz fragments and some fine-grained calcite in a clay matrix. X-ray diffractometer pattern shows quartz, calcite, and clay minerals. This clay appears to have the same geologic structure as the baked clay of Boxes A and B, i.e. the samples examined from Boxes A and B appear to be baked versions of this sample in Box D.

SLAG

Box E (Sample 4 = 65/IV; Sample 6 = 65/IV)

Consists of a number of large (up to 3 in.), irregular, heterogeneous lumps consisting of pieces of white calcite, gray and reddish clay embedded in a foamy black matrix. These lumps appear to be slag, grading into baked clay in some lumps. This baked clay has holes and furrows in the surface, as if straw might have been present at one time. Thin sections of the slag show a glassy, highly vesicular structure containing partially melted crystals of quartz and feldspar. Calcite is also present, as well as clay fragments, which greatly resemble the baked clay specimens described above. Similar minerals are present. X-ray diffractometer patterns of the slag show quartz, traces of feldspar and calcite, and iron and iron aluminum silicates.

METAL

Box C (Samples 5/IV; 109/IV)

2 metal objects:
5/IV appears to be portion of handle.
109/IV–irregularly shaped copper lump covered with green corrosion. Cut surface is bright copper color; small bits of slag can be seen under the microscope embedded near the surface of the metal.

MIXED GROUP

Box H

Sample 9 (36/IV)–excellent X-ray diffractometer pattern for hematite (pigment).
Sample 10 (53/IV)–fine grained clay and calcite mixed.
Sample 11 (80/IV)–red clay with alternating bedding layers of very fine and slightly coarser particles, similar to varves in glacial clays.

Box I

Sample 13 (62/IV)–clay and fine sand with calcite.

Conclusions

Sand and clay have good refractory properties, that is they are relatively stable to elevated temperatures, and therefore may be used in metallurgical processes in several ways:

1. The furnace used for reducing the ore may be constructed of sand bonded with clay.
2. The crucibles for melting the metal are usually ceramic.
3. Molding sands (composed essentially of sand and clay) are used to shape the metal in the casting process.

This group of fragments from Zawi Chemi Shanidar strongly suggests that they were employed in some capacity in the production of copper metal from its ore.

Geologically, the unbaked clay and the baked clay are apparently the same. The size and shape of the sand grains and the variety of minerals present are very similar for the samples examined.

Some samples of baked clay contain small, cylindrical cavities, as if straw were originally present. Organic substances, such as ground bituminous coal or cereal binders, are frequently used even today in sand-clay foundry molding mixtures to impart certain properties. Chopped straw is also used in making bricks.

The high iron content of the clay samples is indicated by the yellowish to reddish colors; yellow and red soils indicate good drainage and are therefore characteristic of dry climates. The terracotta color typical of baked clay is produced by oxidation of the iron present. Yellow ferrous iron is converted to red ferric iron by heating in the presence of oxygen. When oxygen is not present, heating produces gray to black iron oxide.

The black, heterogeneous slag contains small lumps of clay, white lumps which analyze as calcium carbonate, and many cavities produced by escaping gases. These indicate that the copper ore was a sulfide-type ore composed largely of copper sulfide ore minerals, which contain copper combined with sulfur, arsenic, and antimony. Iron, nickel, and cobalt sulfides are common associated minerals in copper sulfide ores. The copper must be freed from these accompanying elements.

The first step in reducing such an ore is "roasting", or heating strongly in air, which converts the metal sulfides to oxides. Arsenic and antimony oxides are volatilized by further heating and the sulfur oxide passes off as a gas.

The roasted ore, now largely copper oxide contaminated with iron sulfides, is melted and treated with silica and lime. This process, known as "slagging", removes the iron. The silica was added most probably in the form of natural sand. Lime is easily obtained from heating crushed limestone. The chemical reaction involved is:

$$2\ FeS + 3O_2 + 2\ SiO_2 \longrightarrow 2\ FeSiO_3 + 2\ SO_2$$

iron sulfide + oxygen + silica sand ⟶ iron silicates (found in slag) + sulfur dioxide gas

Use of the natural sand and lime, rather than pure silica, results in the formation of complex silicates such as iron aluminum silicates, calcium aluminum silicates, in the slag. Unused lumps of clay remain in the glassy slag. Unused lime is rapidly converted by the action of air into calcium carbonate, the white lumps found in the slag. The escaping sulfur dioxide gas forms bubbles in the molten slag.

The copper oxide formed by roasting and slagging reacts with residual copper sulfide to form copper metal. Further sulfur dioxide is given off in the process:

$$2\ Cu_20 + Cu_2S \longrightarrow 6\ Cu + S0_2$$

copper oxide + copper sulfide ⟶ copper metal + sulfur dioxide gas

Small particles of glassy slag were found embedded near one surface of the small copper pellet examined, showing that the metal was produced by a process such as that described above.

The fact that in some samples the slag appeared to grade off into baked clay suggests that the samples examined formed part of a reaction vessel rather than a clay mold for casting.

Elements Found Spectral Lines	Baked Clay	Unbaked Clay	Slag	Clay Calcite	Clay Layers
Al 3082.2 Al 3092.7	> .1	> .1	> .1	> .1	> .1
B 2496.8 B 2497.7	~ .01	.025	~ .01	.011	< .01
Cr 4254.4 Cr 4274.8	> .1	.070	> .1	.0140	.03
Cu 3247.5 Cu 3274.0	> .1	.017	~ .1	.071	.029
Fe 2599.4 Fe 2755.7	> .1	> .1	> .1	> .1	> .1
Mn 2593.7 Mn 2794.8	> .1	> .1	> .1	> .1	.062
Ni 3414.8	.054	.013	.042	.0135	.01
Si 2519.2 Si 2881.6	> .1	> .1	> .1	> .1	> .1
Ti 3372.8 Ti 3653.5	> .1	> .1	> .1	> .1	> .1
Tl 3229.8	> .1	> .1	> .1	> .1	> .1

Spectrographic Analyses

Si, Al major elements in clays (aluminum silicates).
Reddish to orange colors of samples indicates presence of considerable iron.

Iron minerals probably present are:

1. Chiefly limonite and/or hematite (iron oxides)
2. Lesser amounts of ilmenite (iron-titanium oxide)
3. Traces of chromite (iron-chromium oxide)

Study of the comparative analyses of boron, chromium, copper, and nickel in baked clay, unbaked clay, and slag are interesting. The amount of boron (present as borate) in the baked clay and slag has been decreased relative to the amount originally present in the unbaked clay through volatilization brought about by high temperatures.

The amounts of chromium, copper and nickel are higher in the slag and baked clay as a result of the chemical reactions involved in the separation of the metal from its ore.

APPENDIX III

ANALYSE POLLINIQUE DE ZAWI CHEMI

Arlette Leroi-Gourhan

Située dans le Kurdistan irakien, à environ 800 m. d'altitude, la station préhistorique de Zawi Chemi a fait l'objet d'une fouille dés 1956 par R. Solecki (5). Avec l'analyse pollinique du site, deux problémes sont principalement abordés:

- –son environnement pendant l'époque de la culture protonéolithique, dans le cadre des Monts Zagros.
- –la question des graminées de "type Cerealia".

Le diagramme (fig. 17) est en deux parties, toute la base étant contemporaine de l'industrie étudiée par R. Solecki, débutant à l'extrême fin du Pleistocene et se poursuivant au début de l'Holocene. La partie haute du diagramme comprend deux périodes récentes qui seraient peut-être à placer au VI e et XII e siècles aprés J.C. d'apres les objets trouvés.

Une date de C. 14 (10870±300 = 8.920 B.C.) a été fournie concernant le niveau protonéolithique. Cet échantillon ayant été situé dans un carré different du carré de la colonne pollinique, la date n'a pas été portée sur le diagramme, la corrélation n'étant pas possible, étant donné le pendage des couches. Nous avons recu des échantillons de sédiment provenant de plusieurs points de la fouille; par sécurité stratigraphique, nous nous sommes restreints a la seule série verticale continue, dans le carré B. 4; seuls, proches, deux échantillons du C 4 ont été incorporés.

Pour juger de l'environnement végétal de Zawi Chemi, il est nécessaire de ne point oublier certaines difficultés inhérentes à l'analyse pollinique. L'image botanique exacte d'une localité ne peut jamais être donnée, déjà due au taux de pollinisation différent d'une plante à l'autre. Par ailleurs, le lieu même de prélèvement joue un rôle important: dans un lac, il y aura excès des pollens lointains apportés par le vent ou de ceux que les petites rivières auront récoltés le long de leur cours; dans un site terrestre comme Zawi Chemi, le problème est inversé et ce sont les petites herbacées locales qui seront en excédent, l'habitat ayant obligatoirement favorisé un certain déboisement. Il n'en reste pas moins que si les pollens analysés donnent ainsi une image incomplète de l'environnement à cette altitude et à cette époque, la base en est précieuse par des renseignements déjà importants et permettant des comparaisons avec d'autres sites ou d'autres périodes.

L'ensemble de la flore de Zawi Chemi se présente comme une steppe-savane, sèche, avec fort peu d'arbres, les pollens de ceux-ci n'atteignant même pas 3%. La durée de l'occupation Proto-Néolithique n'est pas connue; R. Solecki écrit: "L'étude de la faune recueillie *dans la partie supérieure* de la couche semble indiquer la domestication du mouton" (5, p. 409). Ceci montre que, du point de vue du niveau culturel, une certaine évolution a eu lieu et que, par conséquent, une période très courte ne peut être envisagée. Du point de vue de la végetation, si le couvert des arbres de change guère, la flore herbacée montre 3 phases différenciées, dont la courbe des Chenopodiacées indique les limites. A la base, celles-ci sont rares et les autres espèces peu variées. A partir de 2.21 m., les Chenopodiacées augmentent, ce qui devrait indiquer la sècheresse, point contredit par le développement de plusieurs plantes nouvelles. Le haut de la séquence, de 1.90 m. à 0.90 m. indique une nouvelle phase avec réduction des Chenopodiacées, les Composées liguliflores y étant dominantes.

Il n'est pas question de déduire des fluctuations climatiques de ces seuls éléments; de plus, il y a là un habitat humain, avec tout ce que cela peut comporter comme modification du milieu naturel. Déjà, il se produit automatiquement un certain déboisement et une augmentation des plantes ruderales autour d'un habitat. De plus, si la domestication du mouton s'avère exacte pour la partie finale de l'occupation proto-néolithique, il est évident qu'un paturage, même très restreint dans l'année, aura changé la végétation herbacée: les plantes sont choisies par les animaux et un grand nombre d'entre elles, comme les graminées, avant même la floraison.

Reste une question difficile: le développement, à partir de 2.20 m. des Graminées de "type céréale". Il est utile de faire remarquer que ces pollens se disséminent peu et que, sauf au milieu d'un champ cultivé, les pourcentages s'en trouvent toujours assez faibles. Il est impossible, par la palynologie de différencier les graminées, sauvages, ancêtre de nos céréales, de ces dernières, cultivées. Si, dans un gisement se présente une augmentation des pollens de "type céréale", deux causes peuvent être évoquées:

–soit un changement climatique
–soit des techniques agricoles

Dans le diagramme de Zawi Chemi, des changements apparaissent dans la végétation, mais ils sont mineurs et il est difficile de leur donner une valeur suffisante pour avoir provoquer un développement continu des graminées de "type céréale".

La second hypothèse serait celle d'une proto-agriculture ou de l'introduction de techniques agricoles (1). Ceci apparait comme possible et l'analyse pollinique du niveau proto-néolithique de la grotte de Shanidar, où le "type céréale" prend une grande importance, appuierait cette proposition.

Il n'y a pratiquement plus de pollens de céréales dans la partie supérieure du diagramme, donc pas de champ cultivé aux abords du site, ce qui explique sans doute la légère reprise de quelques arbres. Les Composées, dont beaucoup sont refusées par les troupeaux, ont presque totalement envahi les lieux. Il faut remarquer l'absence de pollens de céréales dans les échantillons proches de la surface du sol, démontrant leur non-infiltration, étant donné qu'actuellement, un champ de blé recouvre l'emplacement de Zawi Chemi.

Il est difficile de faire des comparaisons avec d'autre stations, trop rares ou datées avec trop d'imprécision. Dans la grotte de Shanidar, le niveau B 1, daté de 8.650 B.C. est, en principe, contemporain de Zawi Chemi. Il pourrait toutefois comprendre une période un peu plus récente, les pollens de "type céréale" y atteignent 12%.

Des fluctuations climatiques sont certaines pour cette période de transition vers l'Holocene, mais il n'est pas possible de les saisir à Shanidar ou Zawi Chemi. L'analyse pollinique de Zarzi (2), situé sensiblement à la même altitude et à 140 km au sud-est dans les Zagros, est probablement plus ancienne que Zawi Chemi de 3 â 4,000 ans. La flore est celle d'une steppe très sèche et sans doute très froide, presque sans arbres, à Composées liguliflores très dominantes et des "types Céréale" extrêmement rares (4 pour 4.812 pollens). C'est la fin de la période steppique notée au Lac Zéribar à la même période (7).

Du fait de renseignements concernant des stations éloignées et différenciées comme le lac Zéribar, le Ghab, ou Mureybet (7,4,3), il est vraisemblable que l'ensemble du diagramme de Zawi Chemi se situe dans la période d'amélioration climatique du tout début de l'Holocène, se manifestant dans ces stations par une augmentation de température et d'humidité. Dans les quelques exemples d'analyses du Nord des Zagros, la rareté des pollens de "type Céréale" antérieurement au Proto-néolithique implique que leur augmentation est due à un changement important. Ceci pouvant découler d'un fait climatique, ou de techniques agricules. Peut-être les deux sont-ils liés: si il y a eu domestication des plantes, elle est probablement venue d'ailleurs et, à un moment où l'amélioration du climat facilitait l'expansion des plantes céréalières.

Arl. LEROI-GOURHAN

Laboratoire de Palynologie
Musée de l'Homme, 75116, Paris

References to APPENDIX III

1 – LEROI-GOURHAN Arl. (1969) : "Pollen grains of Graminae and Cerealia from Shanidar and Zawi Chemi." in Ucko. The domestication and exploitation of plants and animals. London, p. 143-148.

2 – LEROI-GOURHAN Arl. (1976) : "Les pollens de Zarzi, dans le Kurdistan irakien". *Sumer*

3 – LEROI-GOURHAN Arl. (1976) : Etudes palynologiques des derniers 11.000 ans en Syrie semi-désertique."
Paléorient

4 – NIKLEWSKI J., and VAN ZEIST W. (1970) : "A late quaternary pollen diagram from Northwestern Syria."
Acta Bot. Neerl., 19 (5) p. 737-754.

5 – SOLECKI R. (1964) : "Zawi Chemi Shanidar, a Paleolithic Site in Northern Irak."
Report VIth Intern. Congr. of Quatern., vol. 4, p. 405-412.

6 – SOLECKI R. (1964) : "Milling tools and the Epi-palaeolithic in the Near East."
Etudes sur le Quaternaire dans le monde. *VIIIe Congr. INQUA*, p. 989.

7 – VAN ZEIST W. (1967) : "Late Quarternary vegetation history of Western Iran."
Rev. Palaeobot. Palyn., 2, p. 301-311.

8 – VAN ZEIST W. (1969) : "Reflections on prehistoric environments in the Near East." in Ucko . . . The domestication and exploitation of plants and animals. London, p. 35-46.

BIBLIOGRAPHY

ARKELL, A. J.

1953 *Shaheinab.* Oxford University Press, London.

BARDON, L., and A. & J. BOUYSSONIE

1906 "Outils ecailles par percussion," *Revue de l'Ecole d' Anthropologie de Paris. Revue mensuelle,* Vol. XVI, pp. 170-175.

BRAIDWOOD, R. J., and B. HOWE

1960 *Prehistoric Investigations in Iraqi Kurdistan.* Studies in Ancient Oriental Civilization, 31. University of Chicago Press, Chicago.

CAMPBELL THOMPSON, R., and M. E. L. MALLOWAN

1933 "The British Museum Excavations at Nineveh, 1931-32," *University of Liverpool, Annals of Archaeology and Anthropology,* Vol. XX, pp. 71-186.

COLE, S. M.

1954 "Differentiation of Non-Metallic Tools," in *A History of Technology,* edited by C. Singer, E. J. Holmyard, and A. R. Hall, Vol. I., pp. 459-519. Oxford University Press, New York and London.

CROWFOOT, G. M.

1954 "Textiles, Basketry, and Mats," in *A History of Technology,* edited by C. Singer, E. J. Holmyard, and A. R. Hall, Vol. I., pp. 413-447. Oxford University Press, New York, and London.

DREW, I. M.

1970 "Laboratory Report" in R. L. and R. S. Solecki "Grooved Stones from Zawi Chemi Shanidar, A Protoneolithic Site in Northern Iraq," *American Anthropologist,* Vol. 72, pp. 839-840.

FEREMBACH, D.

1970 "Etude Anthropologique des Ossements Humains Proto-Neolithiques de Zawi Chemi Shanidar," *Sumer,* Vol. XXVI, pp. 21-64.

GARROD, D. A. E., and D. M. A. BATE

1937 *The Stone Age of Mount Carmel*, Vol. I. Clarendon Press, Oxford.

GOULD, R. A., D. A. KOSTER, and A. H. L. SONTZ

1971 "The Lithic Assemblage of the Western Desert Aborigines of Australia," *American Antiquity*, Vol. 36, pp. 149-169.

HELBAEK, H.

1959 "Domestication of Food Plants in the Old World," *Science*, Vol. 130, pp. 365-372.

HENRY, D. O.

1973 *The Natufian of Palestine: Its Material Culture and Ecology*. Dallas.

LEROI-GOURHAN, A.

1969 "Pollen Grains of Gramineae and Cerealia from Shanidar and Zawi Chemi," in *The Domestication and Exploitation of Plants and Animals*, edited by P. J. Ucko and G. W. Dimbleby, pp. 143-148. Duckworth, London.

LEROI-GOURHAN, A.

1976 "Les Pollens de Zarzi, dans le Kurdistan irakien," *Sumer*.

MASON, O. T.

1891 "Aboriginal Skin Dressing," *Annual Report of the U.S. National Museum for 1889*, pp. 553-589.

MASON, O. T.

1904 "Aboriginal American Basketry. Indian Basketry," *Annual Report of the U.S. National Museum for 1902*, pp. 171-548.

MELLAART, J.

1967 *Çatal Hüyük: A Neolithic Town in Anatolia*. Thames and Hudson, London.

PERKINS, D.

1964 "Prehistoric Fauna from Shanidar, Iraq," *Science*, Vol. 144, pp. 1565-1566.

RAINEY, F.

1940 "Archaeological Investigations in Central Alaska," *American Antiquity*, Vol. 5, pp. 299-308.

SKINNER, A.

1911 "Notes on the Eastern Cree and Northern Saulteaux," *American Museum of Natural History Anthropological Papers*, Vol. IX, Part 1.

SKINNER, A.

1921 *Material Culture of the Menomini.* Indian Notes and Monographs. Museum of the American Indian, Heye Foundation, New York.

SLOANE, E.

1974 *A Museum of Early American Tools.* Ballantine Books, New York.

SOLECKI, R. L.

1964 "Zawi Chemi Shanidar, a Post-Pleistocene Village in Northern Iraq," *INQUA, VI International Congress on Quaternary*, Warsaw, 1961, pp. 402-412.

SOLECKI, R. L.

1972 "Milling Tools and the Proto-Neolithic Economy of the Near East," *Proceedings of the VIII INQUA Congress*, Vol. 2, pp. 989-994.

SOLECKI, R. L.

1977 "Predatory Bird Rituals at Zawi Chemi Shanidar," *Sumer*, Vol. XXXIII, pp. 42-47.

SOLECKI, R. L., and R. S. SOLECKI

1963 "Two Hafted Bone Implements from Shanidar, Northern Iraq," *Antiquity*, Vol. 37, No. 145, pp. 58-60.

SOLECKI, R. L., and R. S. SOLECKI

1970 "Grooved Stones from Zawi Chemi Shanidar, A Protoneolithic Site in Northern Iraq," *American Anthropologist*, Vol. 72, pp. 831-841.

SOLECKI, R. S.

1955 "Shanidar Cave, A Paleolithic Site in Northern Iraq," *Smithsonian Annual Report 1954*, pp. 389-425.

SOLECKI, R. S.

1963 "Prehistory in Shanidar Valley, Northern Iraq," *Science,* Vol. 139, pp. 179-193.

SOLECKI, R., and M. RUBIN

1958 "Dating of Zawi Chemi, an Early Village Site at Shanidar, Northern Iraq," *Science,* Vol. 127, p. 1446.

SONNENFELD, J.

1962 "Interpreting the Function of Primitive Implements," *American Antiquity,* Vol. 28, pp. 56-65.

TIXIER, J.

1963 *Typologie de L'Épipaléolithique du Maghreb.* Mémoires du Centre de Recherches Anthropologiques Préhistoriques et Ethnographiques, Alger, No. II. Arts et Métiers Graphiques, Paris.

VAN ZEIST, W.

1967 "Late Quaternary Vegetation History of Western Iran," *Review of Palaeobotany and Palynology,* Vol. 2, pp. 301-311.

VAN ZEIST, W.

1969 "On Macroscopic Traces of Food Plants in Southwestern Asia (With Some Reference to Pollen Data)," *Philosophical Transactions of the Royal Society of London, B,* Vol. 275, pp. 27-41.

VAN ZEIST, W., H. WOLDRING, and D. STAPERT

1975 "Late Quaternary Vegetation and Climate of Southwestern Turkey," *Palaeohistoria,* Vol. 17, pp. 53-143.

VAN ZEIST, W., and H. E. WRIGHT, Jr.

1963 "Preliminary Pollen Studies at Lake Zeribar, Zagros Mountains, Southwestern Iran, *Science,* Vol. 140, pp. 65-67.

WHITE, J. P.

1968 "Fabricators, Outils ecailes or Scalar Cores?," *Mankind,* Vol. 6, pp. 658-666.

WISSLER, C.

1910 "Material Culture of the Blackfoot Indians," *American Museum of Natural History Anthropological Papers,* Vol. V, Part 1.

ERRATA CORRIGE – *BM* 13

Location:	Instead of:	Read:
p. 4, second line from bottom	was	were
p. 12, line 9	perhps	perhaps
p. 25, line 29	addzes	adzes
p. 41, line 1	but	butt
p. 42, line 25	hold	hole

NOTE

For the sake of convenience in printing, Figs. 7 and 17 appear out of sequence: Fig. 17 is printed after Fig. 1, and Fig. 7 is printed after Fig. 9.

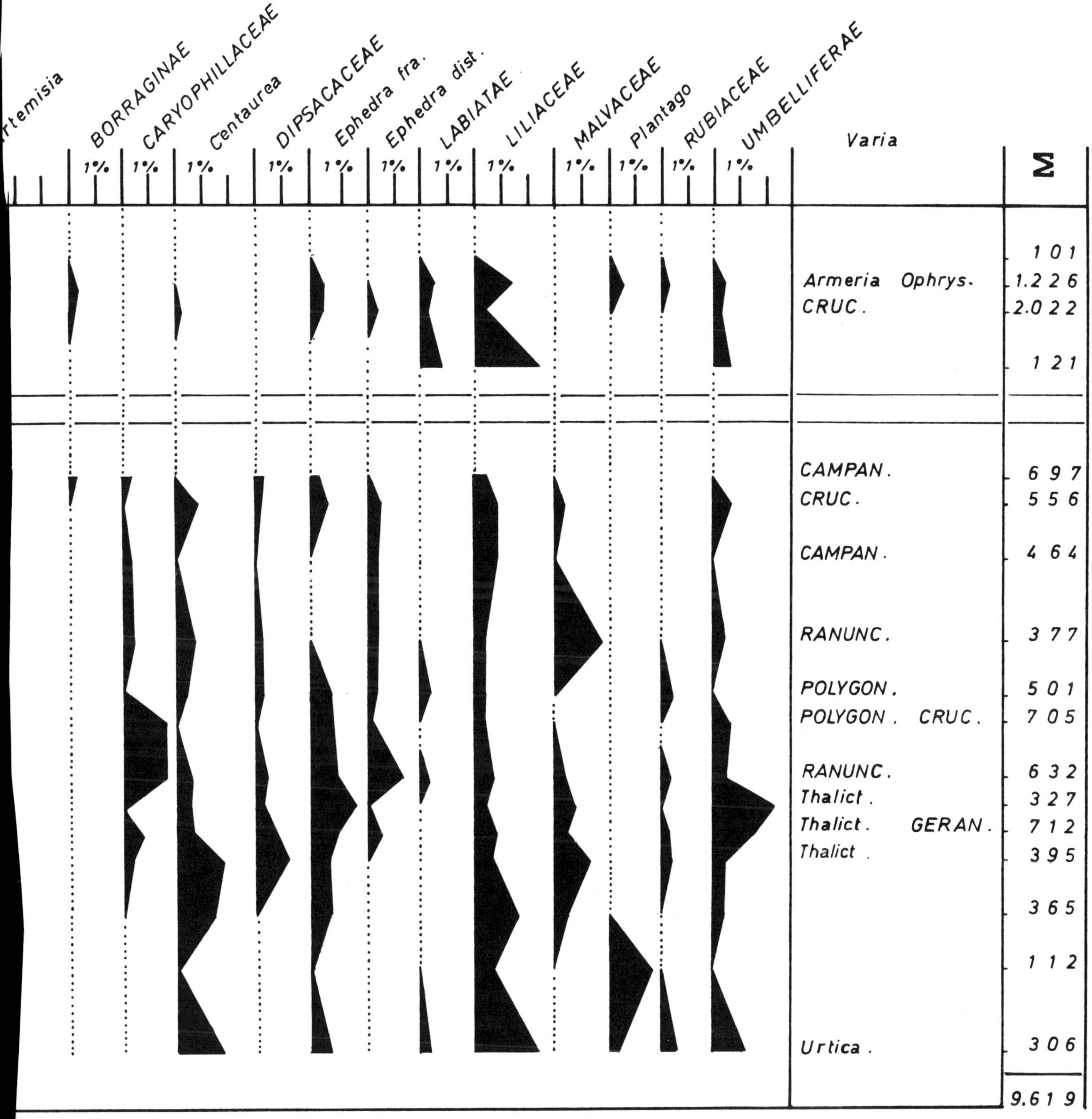

AN. ARL. LEROI-GOURHAN.

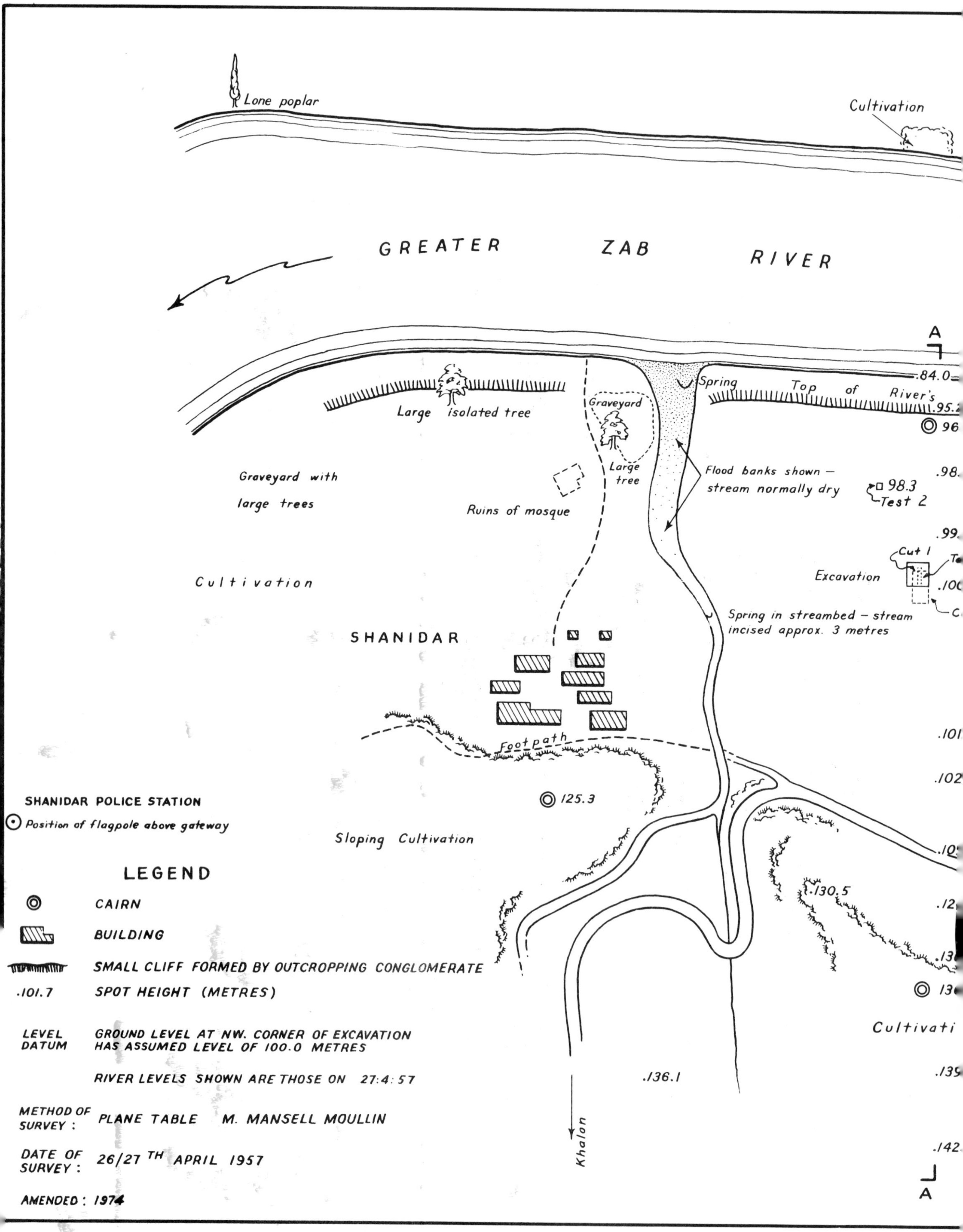
Lone poplar
Cultivation
GREATER ZAB RIVER
A
.84.0
Spring
Top of River's
.95.
96
Large isolated tree
Graveyard
Large tree
Graveyard with large trees
Ruins of mosque
Flood banks shown – stream normally dry
98.3
Test 2
.98.
.99.
Cut I
Excavation
Cultivation
Spring in streambed – stream incised approx. 3 metres
SHANIDAR
Footpath
.101
.102
125.3
SHANIDAR POLICE STATION
Position of flagpole above gateway
Sloping Cultivation
.130.5
LEGEND
CAIRN
BUILDING
SMALL CLIFF FORMED BY OUTCROPPING CONGLOMERATE
.101.7 SPOT HEIGHT (METRES)
LEVEL DATUM
GROUND LEVEL AT NW. CORNER OF EXCAVATION HAS ASSUMED LEVEL OF 100.0 METRES
RIVER LEVELS SHOWN ARE THOSE ON 27:4:57
METHOD OF SURVEY : PLANE TABLE M. MANSELL MOULLIN
DATE OF SURVEY : 26/27 TH APRIL 1957
AMENDED : 1974
.136.1
Khalon
.142.
A
Cultivati

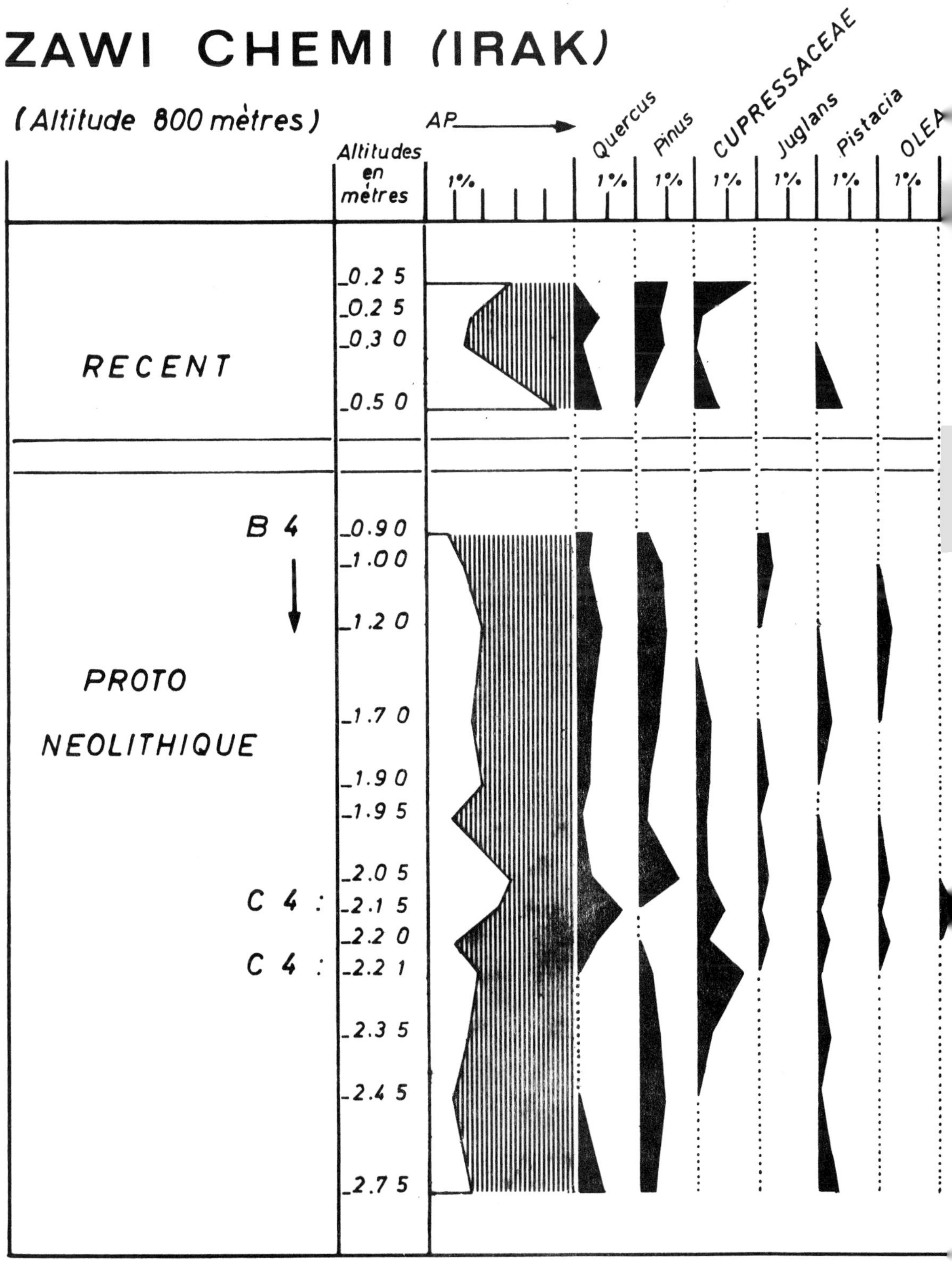

Figure 17. Pollen Diagram for Zawi Chemi Shanidar

Figure 1. Map of Zawi Chemi Shanidar

Type Cerealia
CHENOPODIACEAE
TUBULIFLORAE
LIGULIFLORAE
GRAMINAE
RHAMNACEAE
Alnus
Pterocarya
1%
10%
50%

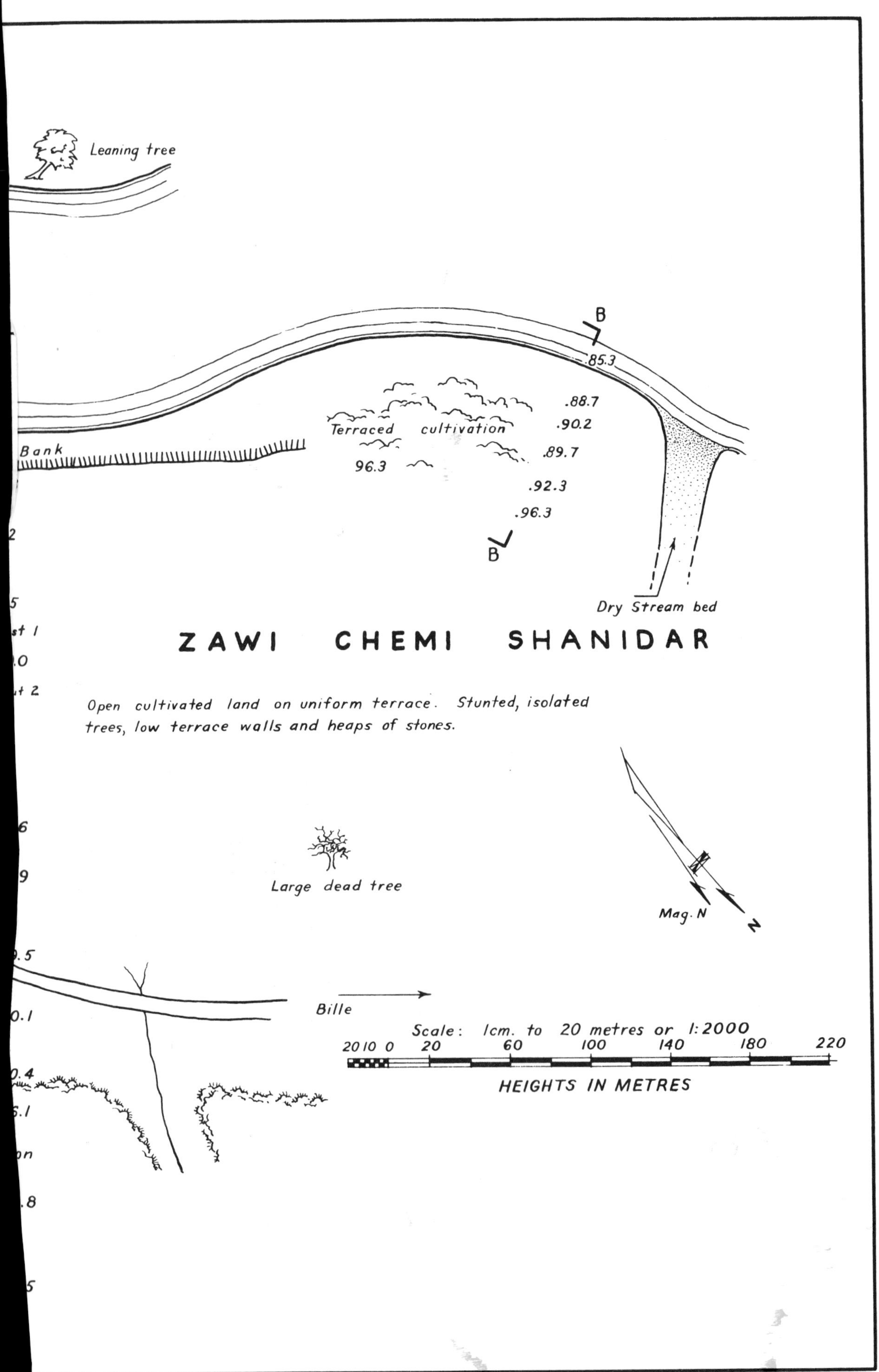

ZAWI CHEMI SHANIDAR
Leaning tree
B
.85.3
.88.7
.90.2
Terraced cultivation
.89.7
96.3
.92.3
.96.3
B
Bank
Dry Stream bed
Open cultivated land on uniform terrace. Stunted, isolated trees, low terrace walls and heaps of stones.
Large dead tree
Mag. N
N
Bille
Scale: lcm. to 20 metres or 1:2000
20 10 0 20 60 100 140 180 220
HEIGHTS IN METRES

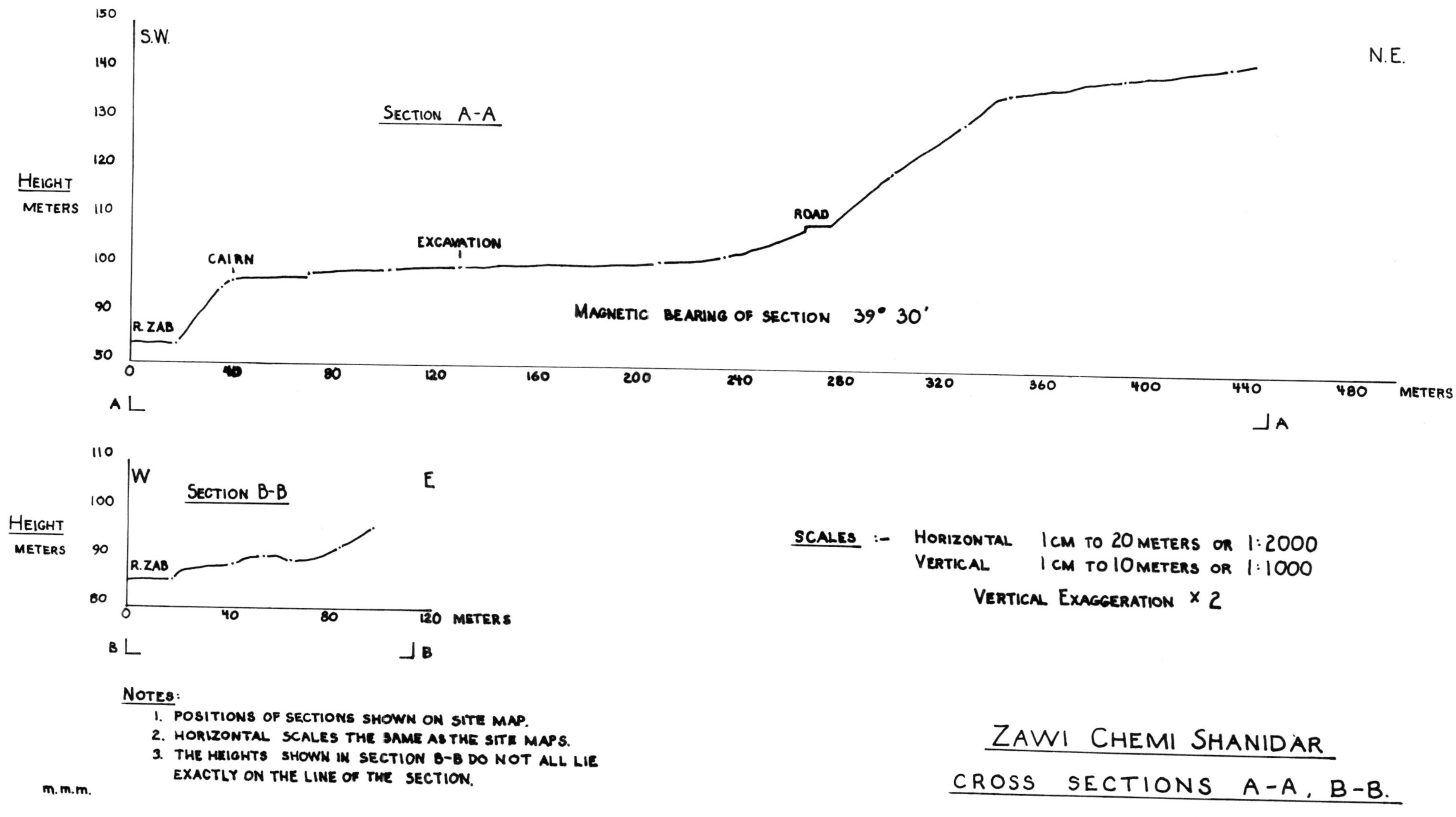

Figure 2. Cross Sections A-A, B-B, Zawi Chemi Shanidar

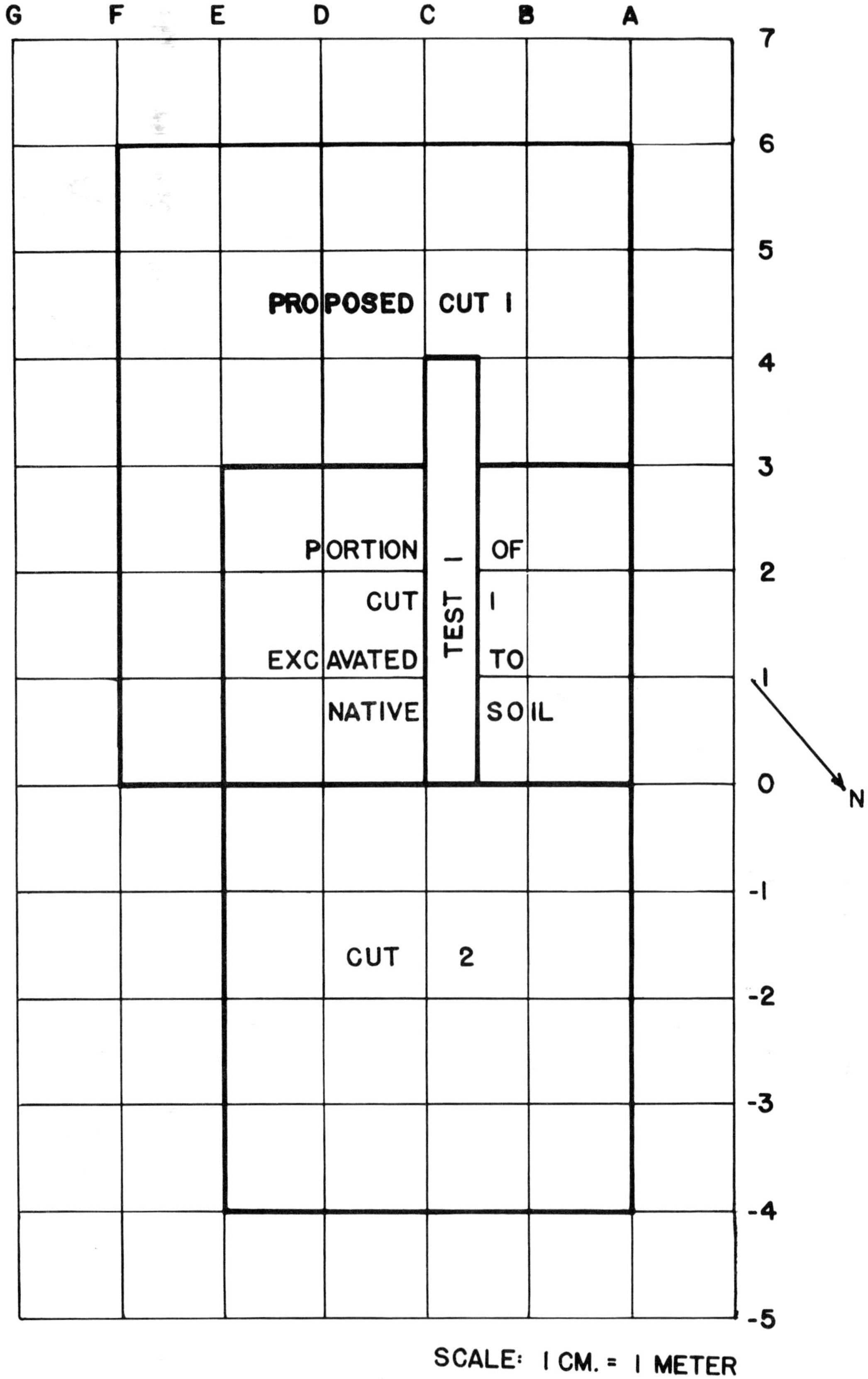

Figure 3. Plan of Excavations of Test 1, and Cuts 1 and 2 at Zawi Chemi Shanidar

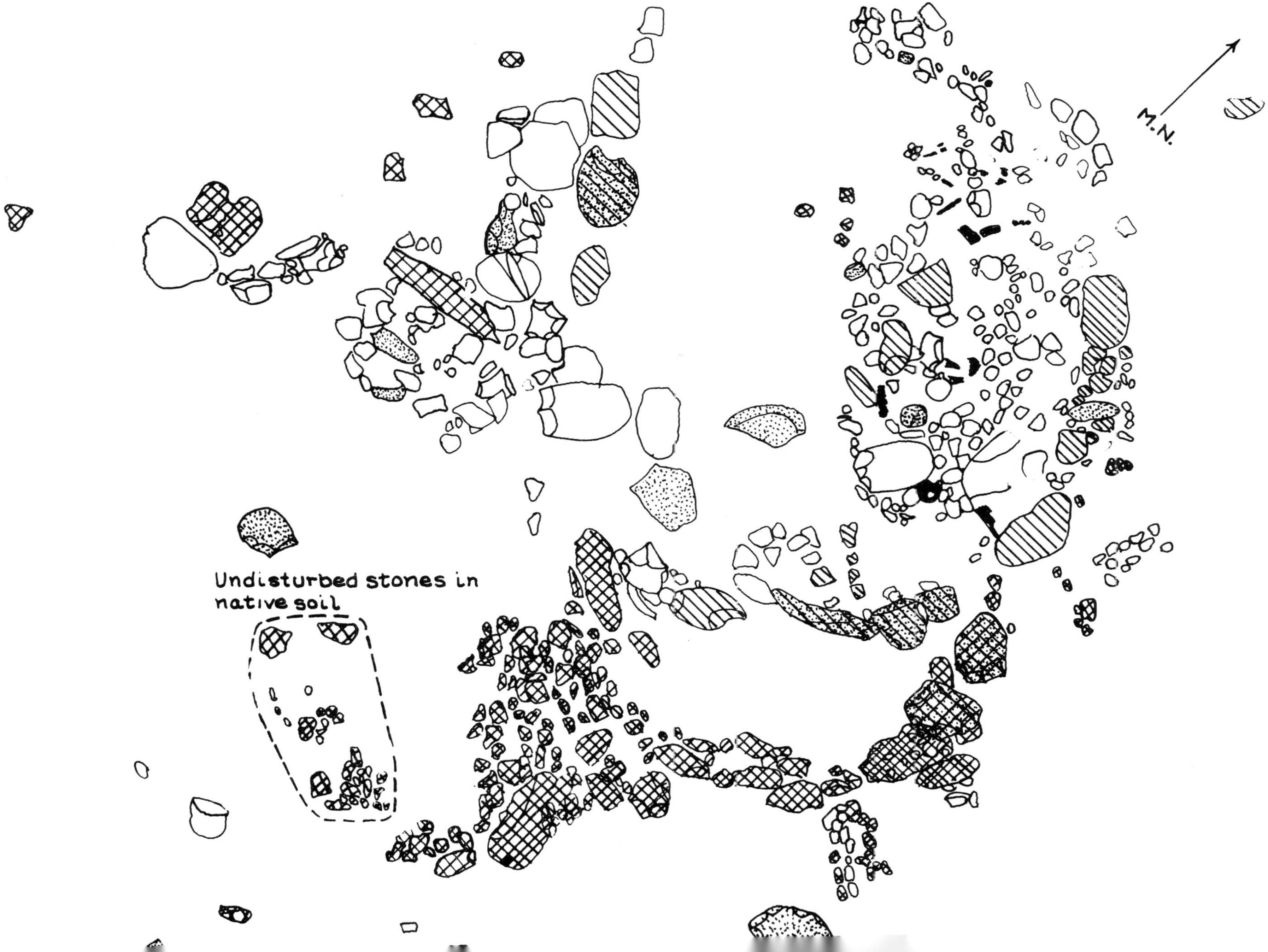
Undisturbed stones in native soil
M.N.

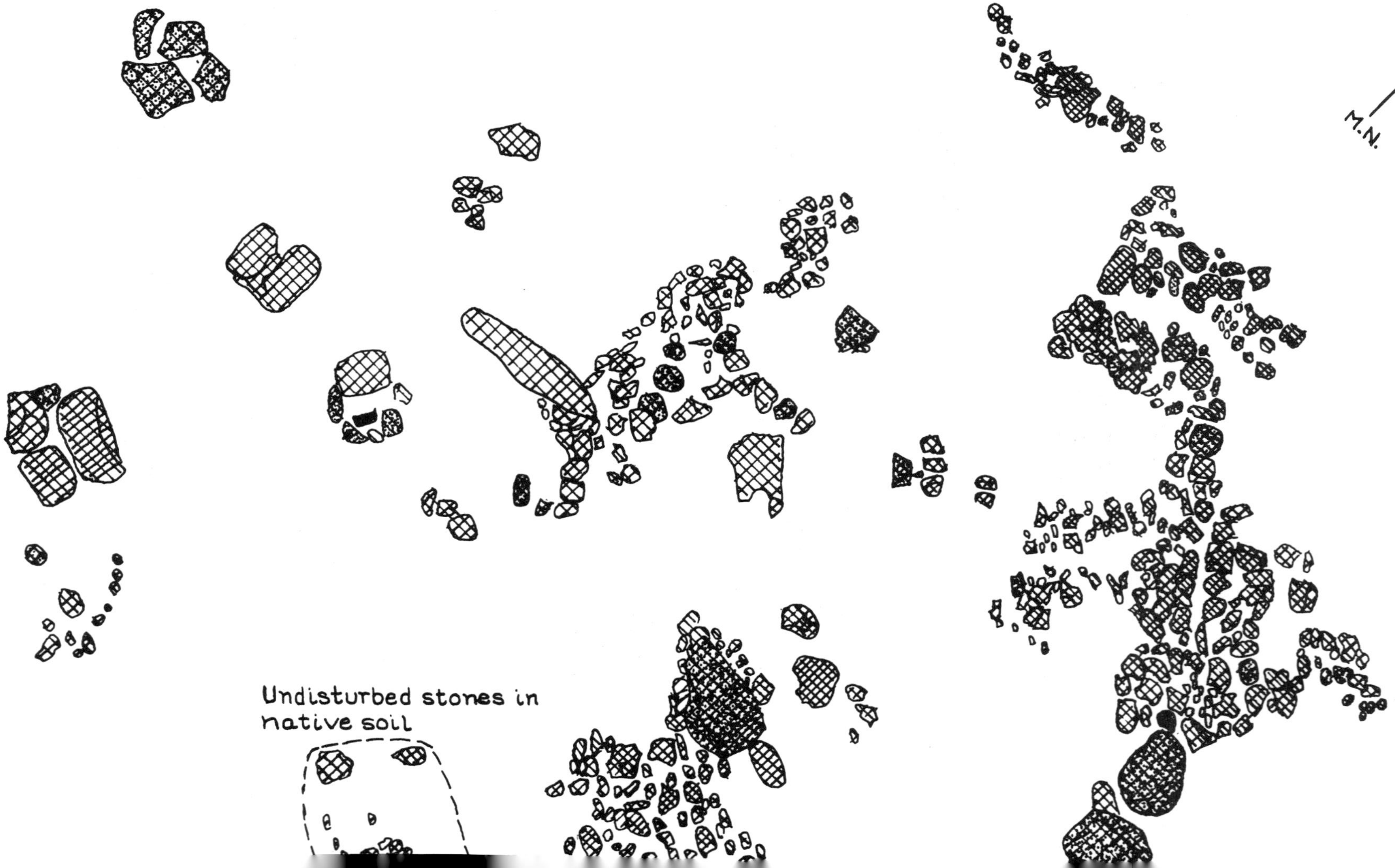

M.N.
Undisturbed stones in native soil

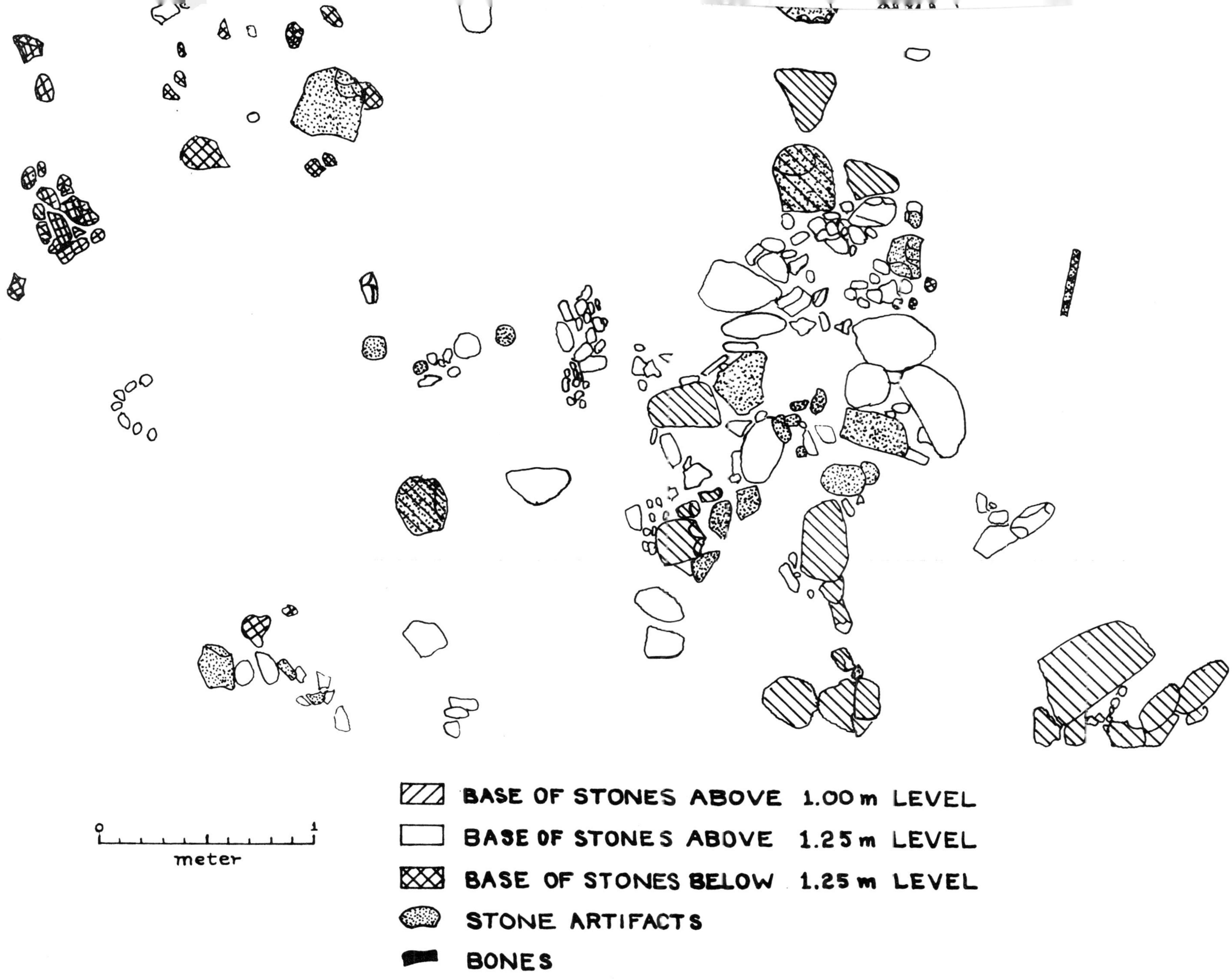

Figure 8. Structure I, Cut 1, at 1.25 Meter Level

Figure 9. Structure I, Cut 1, at 1.50 Meter Level

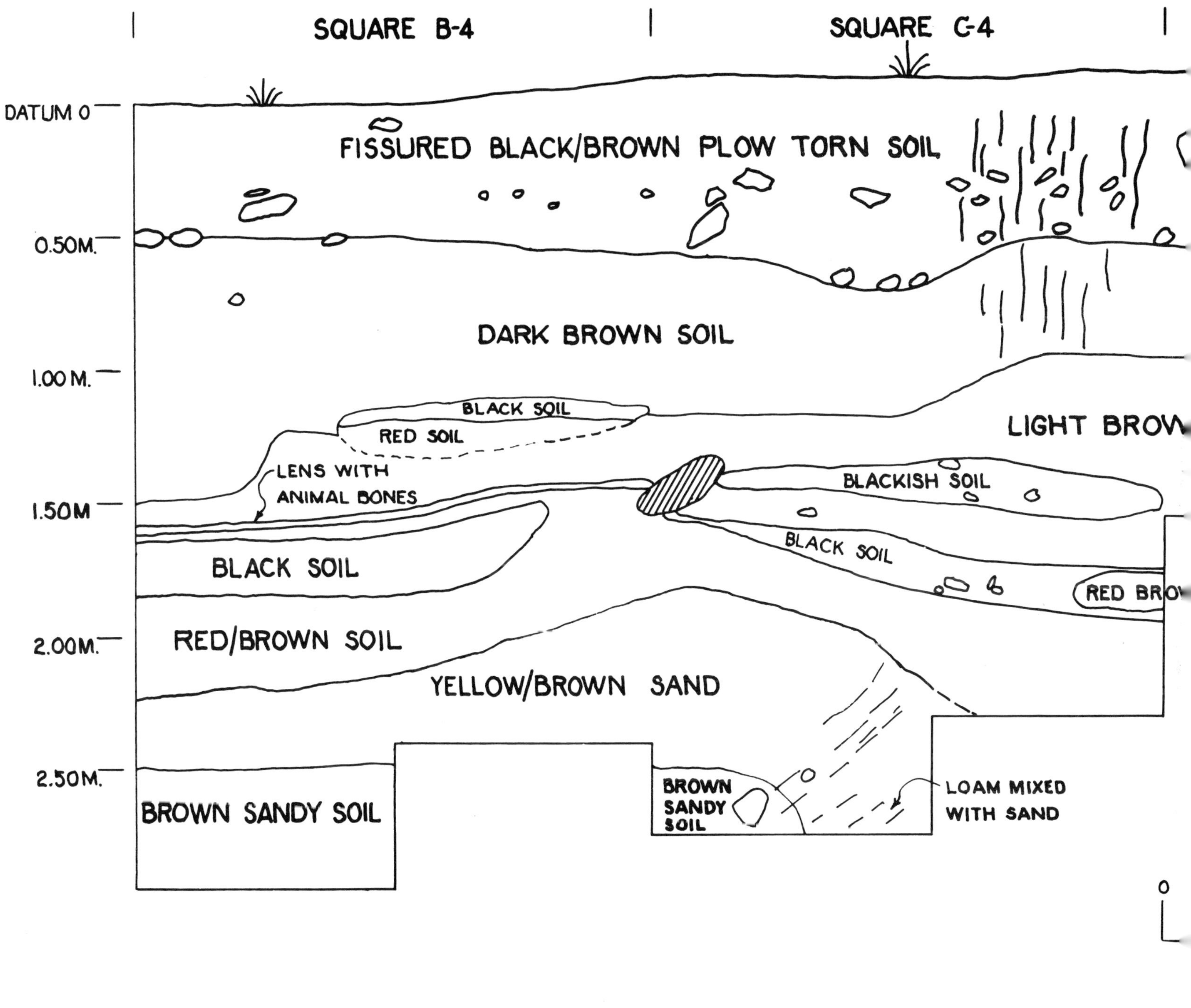

Figure 6. Northeast Wall, C

(For Fig. 7 see after Fig. 9.)

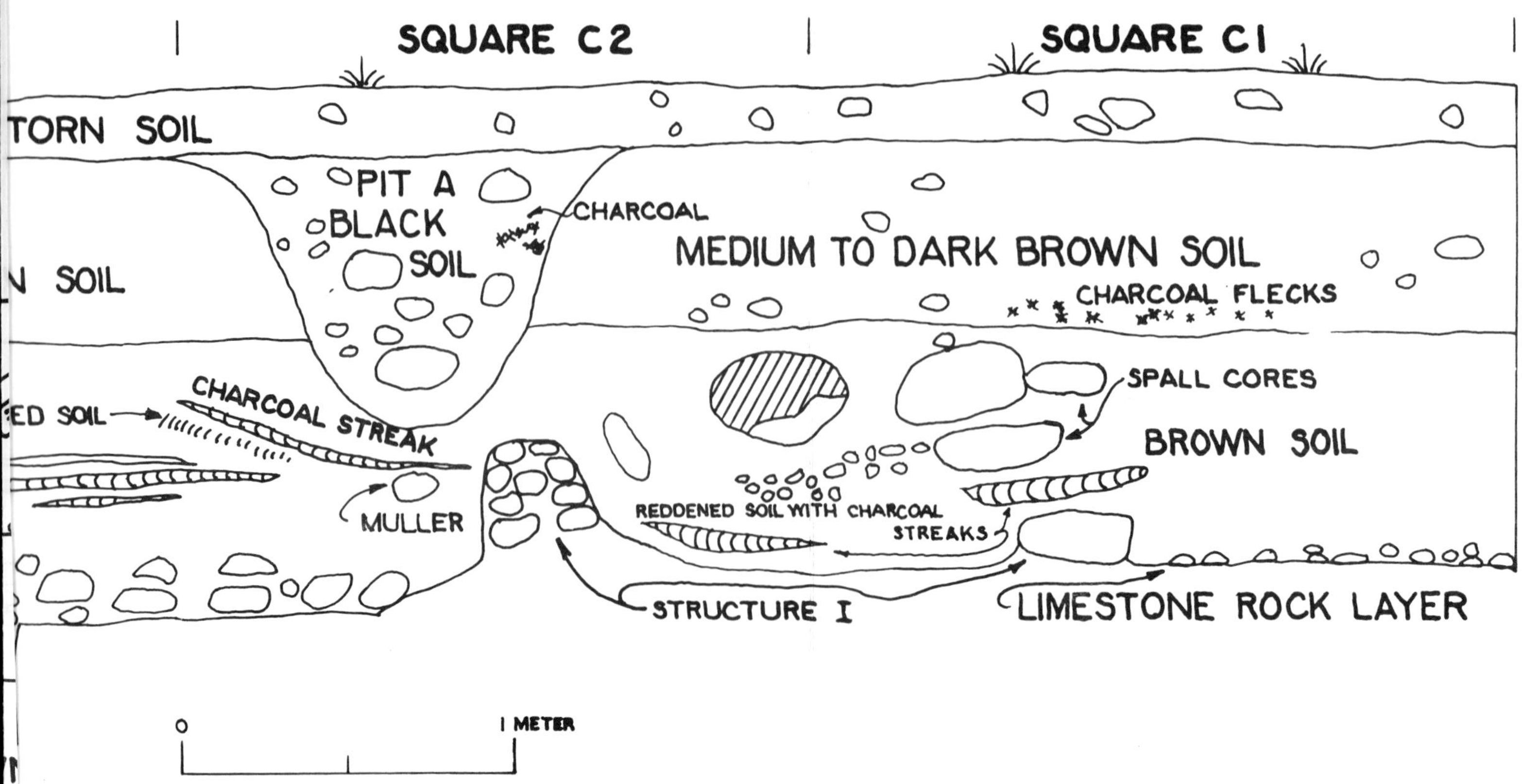
SQUARE C2
SQUARE C1
TORN SOIL
N SOIL
PIT A
BLACK
SOIL
CHARCOAL
MEDIUM TO DARK BROWN SOIL
CHARCOAL FLECKS
ED SOIL
CHARCOAL STREAK
SPALL CORES
BROWN SOIL
MULLER
REDDENED SOIL WITH CHARCOAL
STREAKS
STRUCTURE I
LIMESTONE ROCK LAYER
0
1 METER

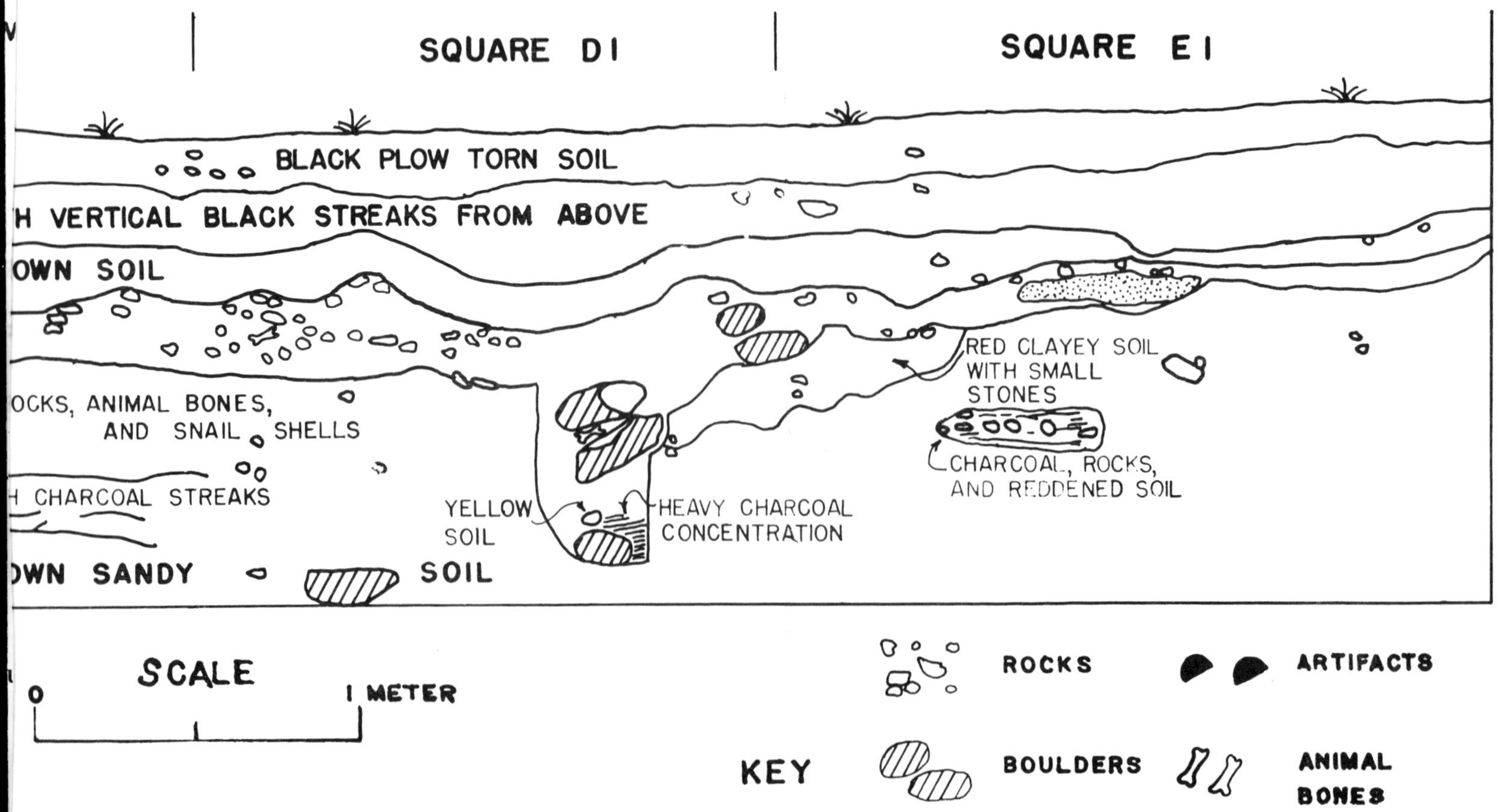
SQUARE D1
SQUARE E1
BLACK PLOW TORN SOIL
H VERTICAL BLACK STREAKS FROM ABOVE
OWN SOIL
RED CLAYEY SOIL
WITH SMALL
STONES
OCKS, ANIMAL BONES,
AND SNAIL SHELLS
CHARCOAL, ROCKS,
AND REDDENED SOIL
H CHARCOAL STREAKS
YELLOW
SOIL
HEAVY CHARCOAL
CONCENTRATION
OWN SANDY
SOIL
SCALE
0
1 METER
ROCKS
ARTIFACTS
KEY
BOULDERS
ANIMAL
BONES

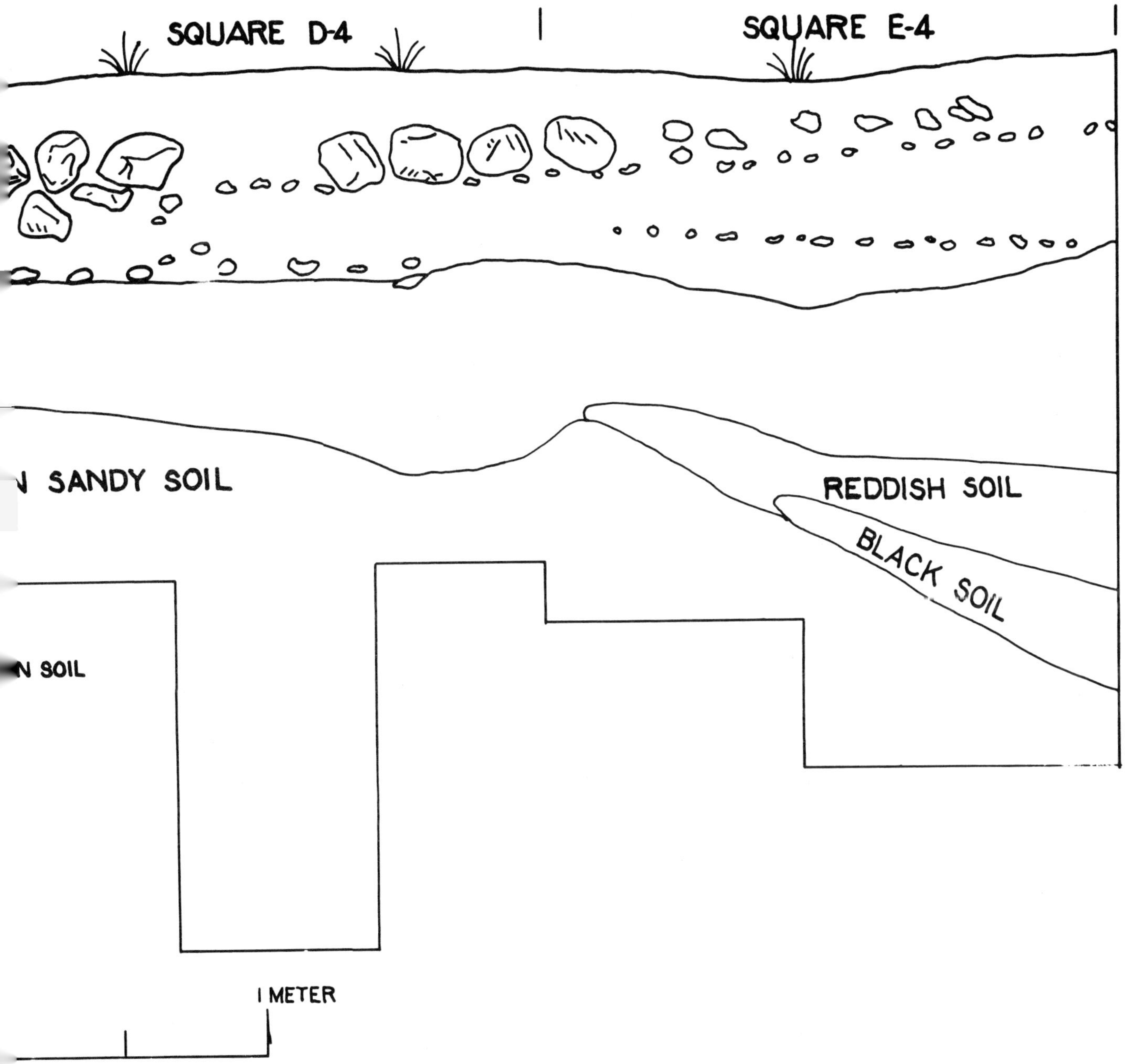
SQUARE D-4
SQUARE E-4
N SANDY SOIL
REDDISH SOIL
BLACK SOIL
N SOIL
I METER

ıt 2

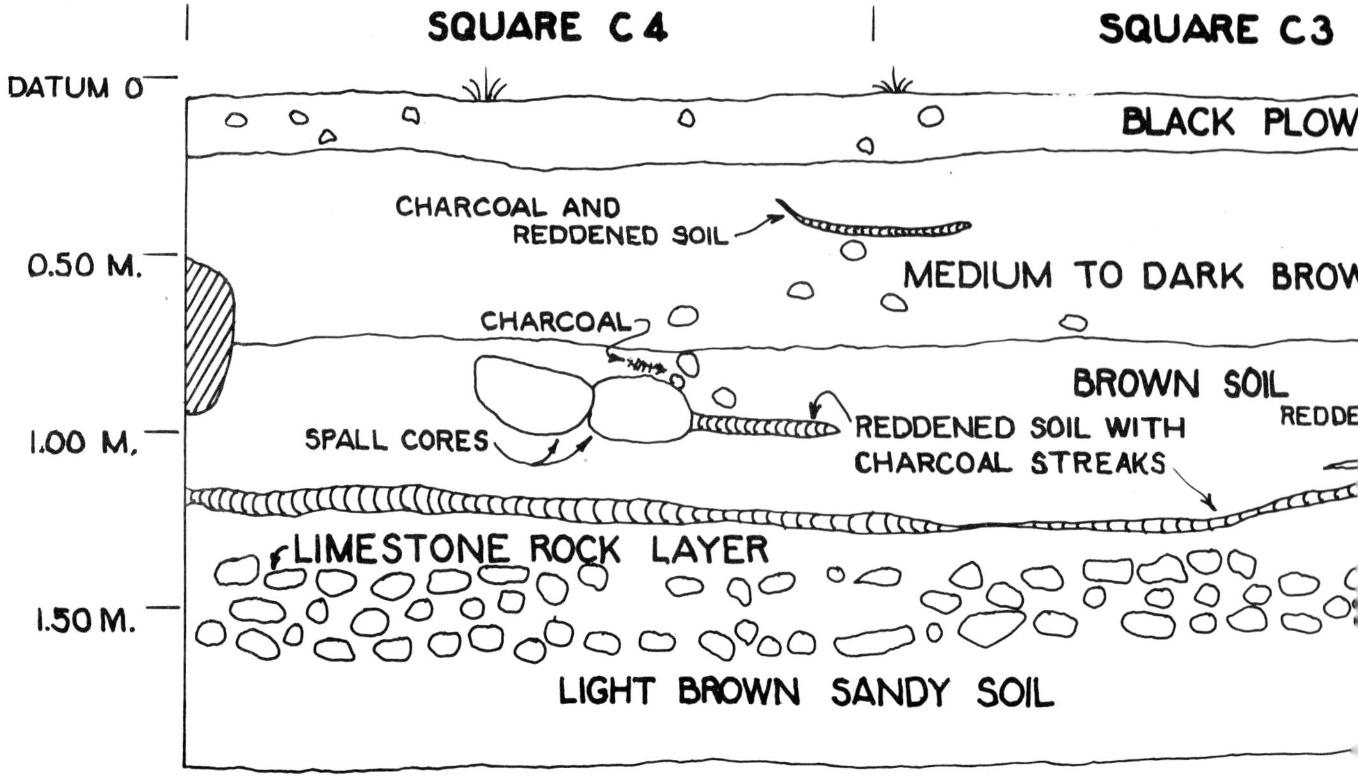

Figure 4. Northwest Wall, Test 1

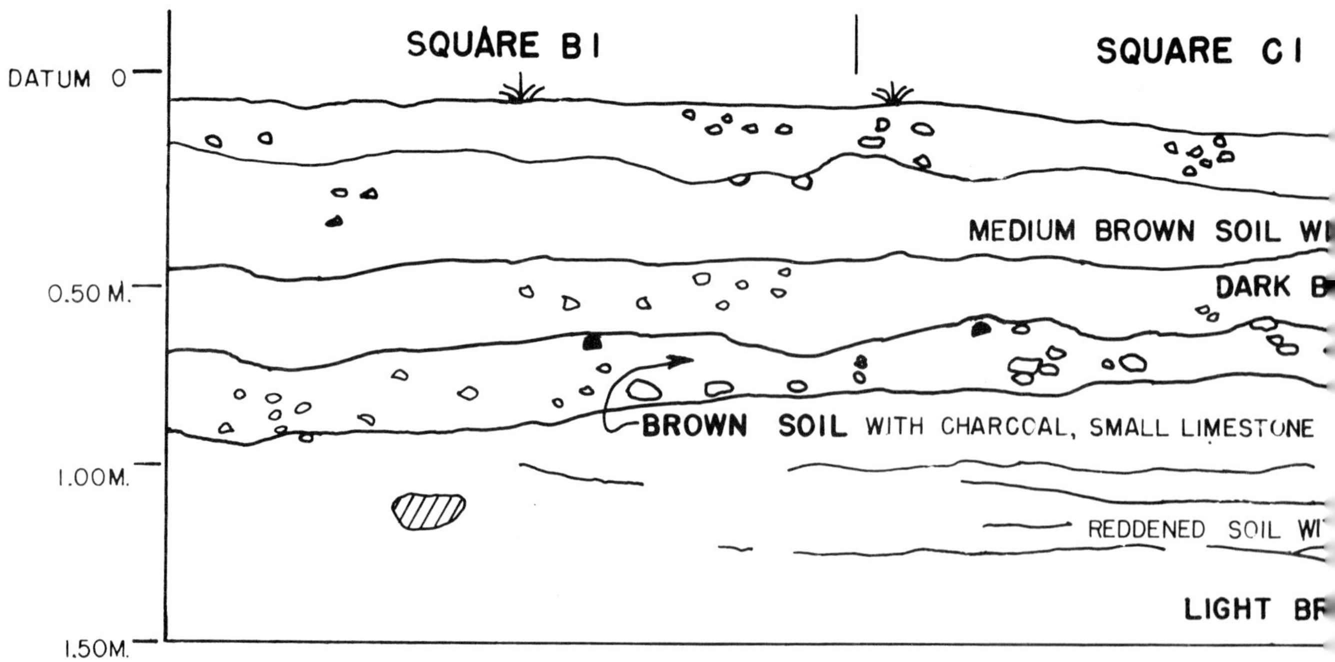

Figure 5. Northeast Wall, Cut 1

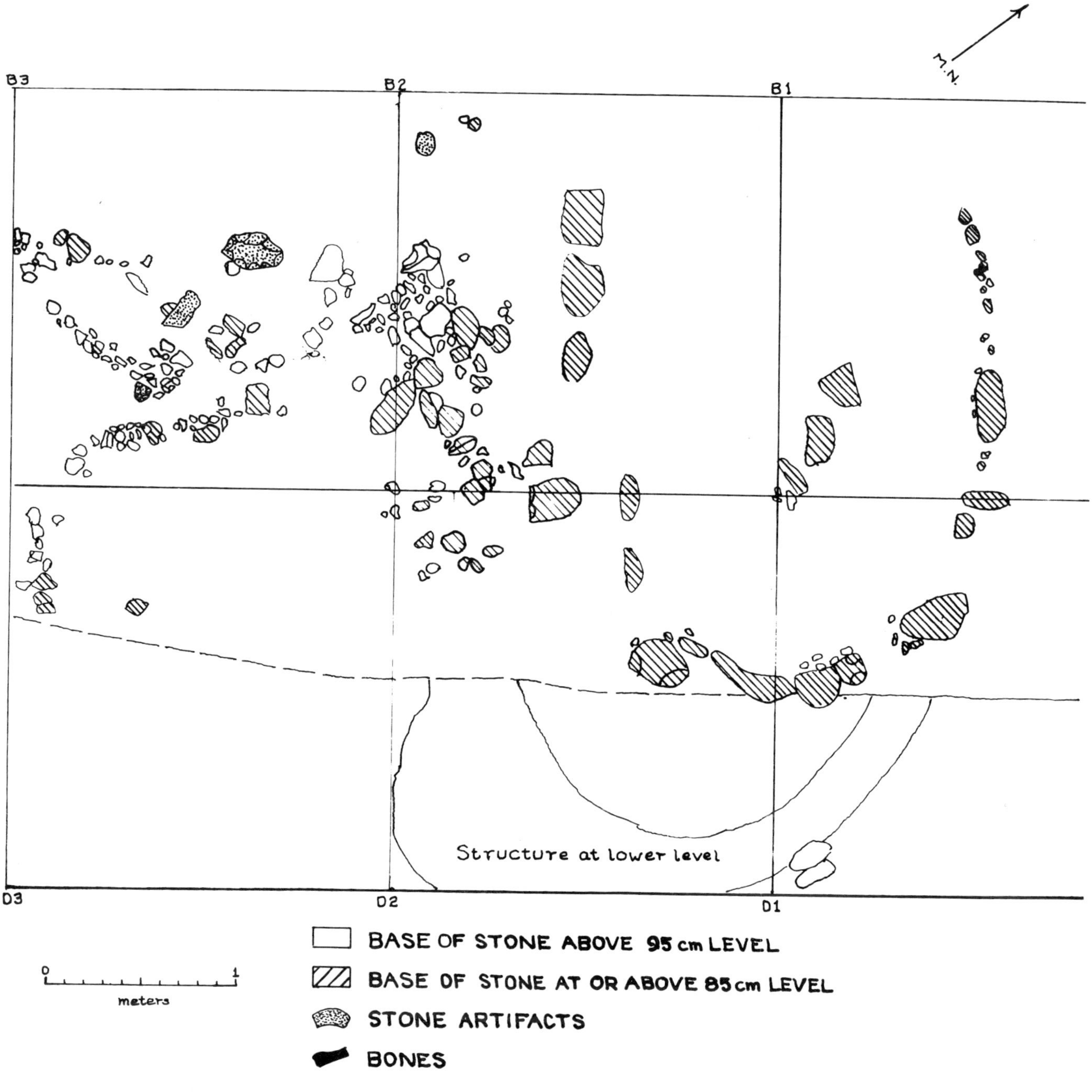

Figure 7. Structure I, Cut 1, at .95 Meter Level

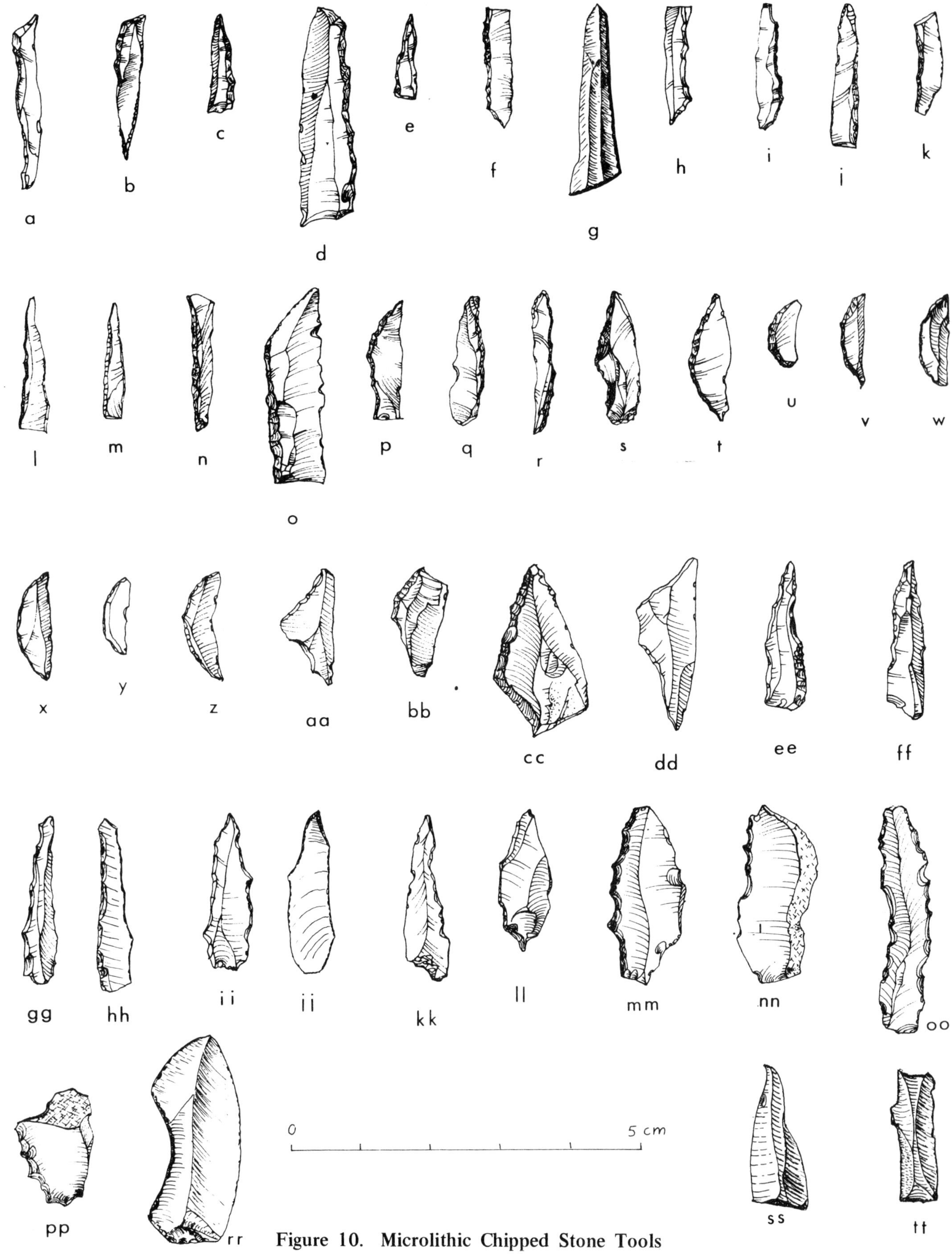

Figure 10. Microlithic Chipped Stone Tools

a-s, Backed blades. t-z, Lunates. aa,bb, Triangles. cc, Incomplete triangle. dd, Trapezoid. ee-kk, Borers. ll, Burin. mm-pp, Denticulates. qq, Notched piece. rr,ss, Truncated pieces.

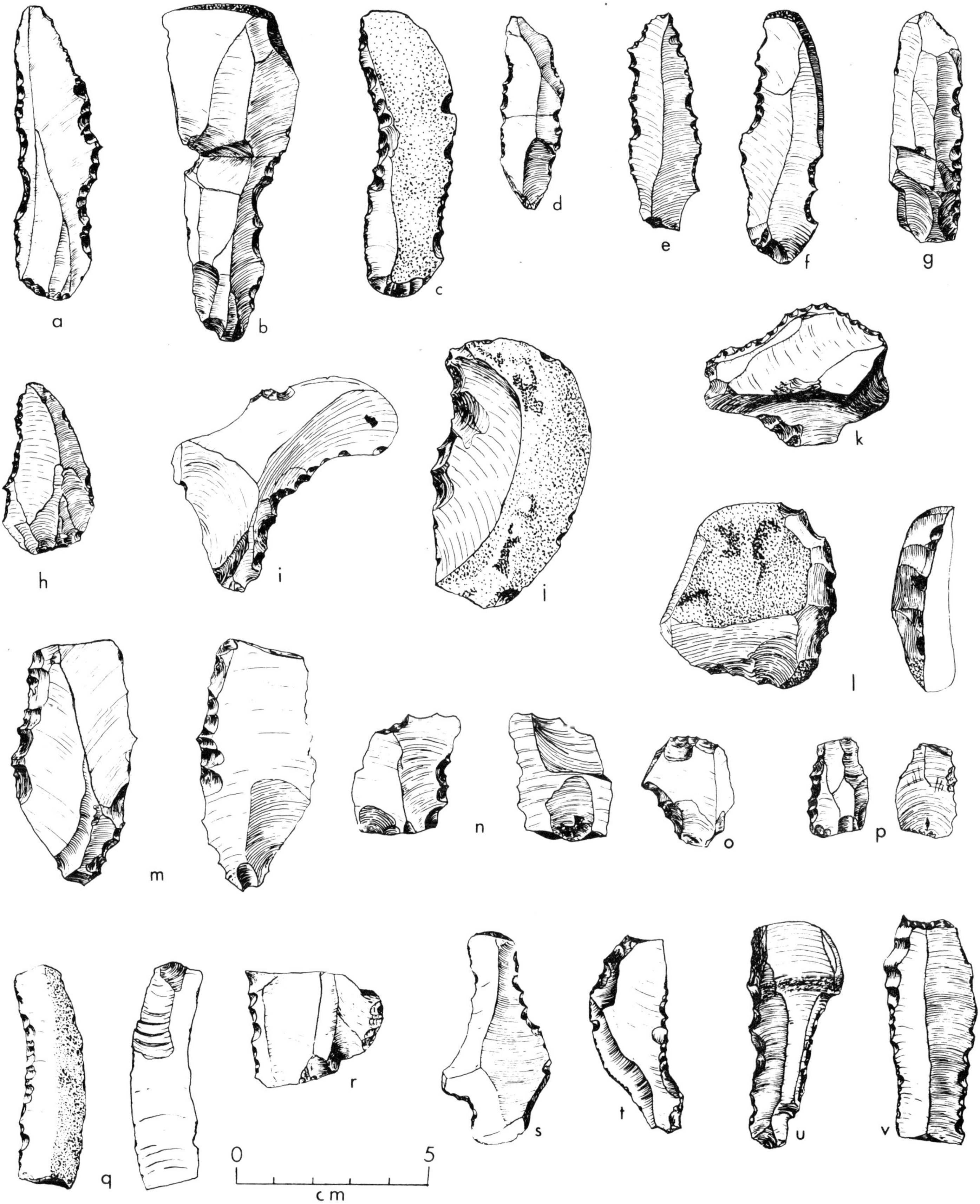

Figure 11. Denticulate Tools

a-l, Simple. m, Alternate. n-p, On pièces esquillées. q,r, With snapped ends. s, And notched. t, And notched and end scraper. u, And side scraper. v, And end scraper.

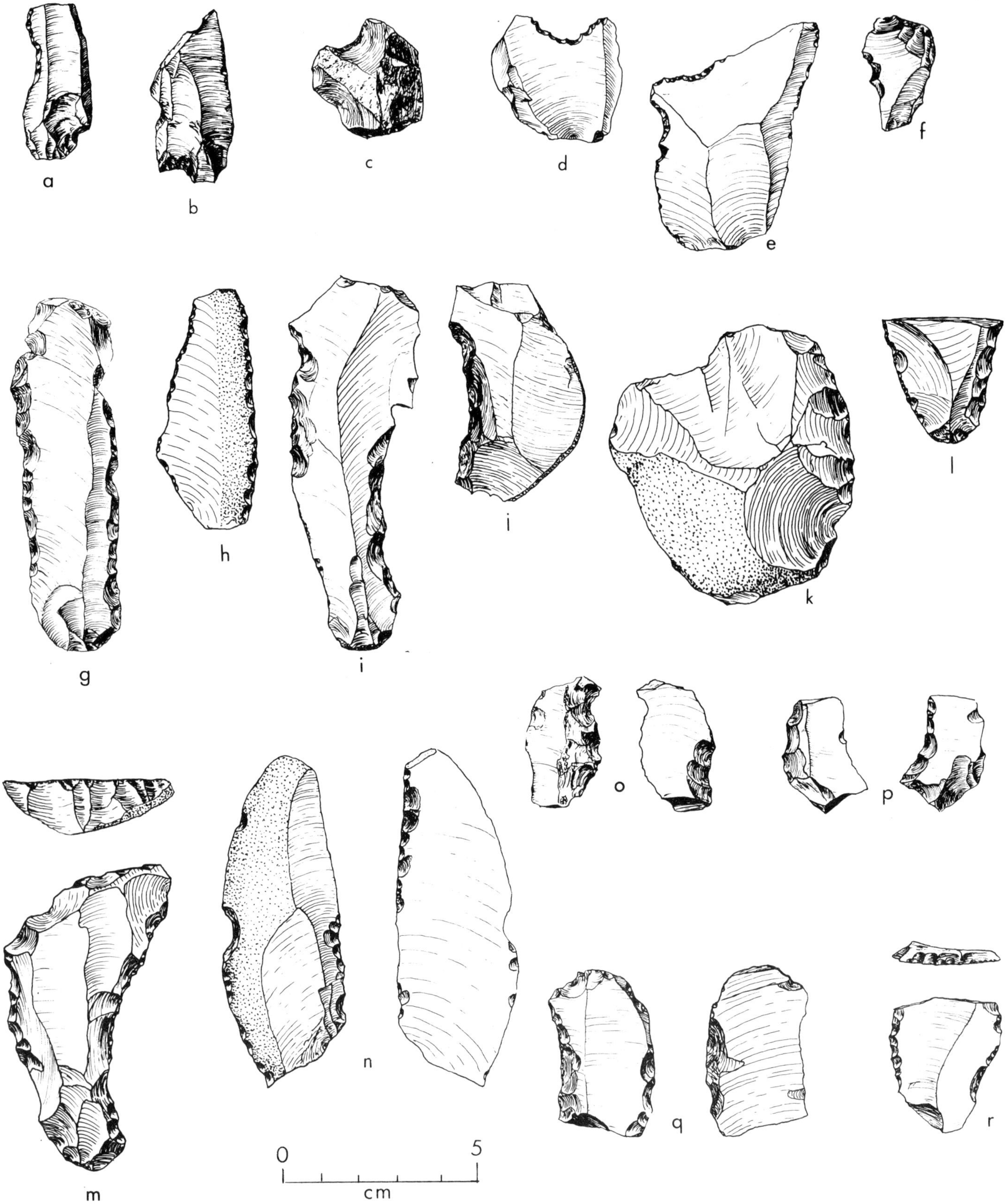

Figure 12. Notched Pieces and Side Scrapers

a-e, Notched pieces, simple. f, Notched piece, on a piece esquillee. g,h, Side scrapers, simple. i-l, Side scrapers, heavy. m, Side scraper, heavy and end scraper. n-p, Side scrapers, alternate. q, Side scraper, bifacial. r, Side scraper, on a truncated piece.

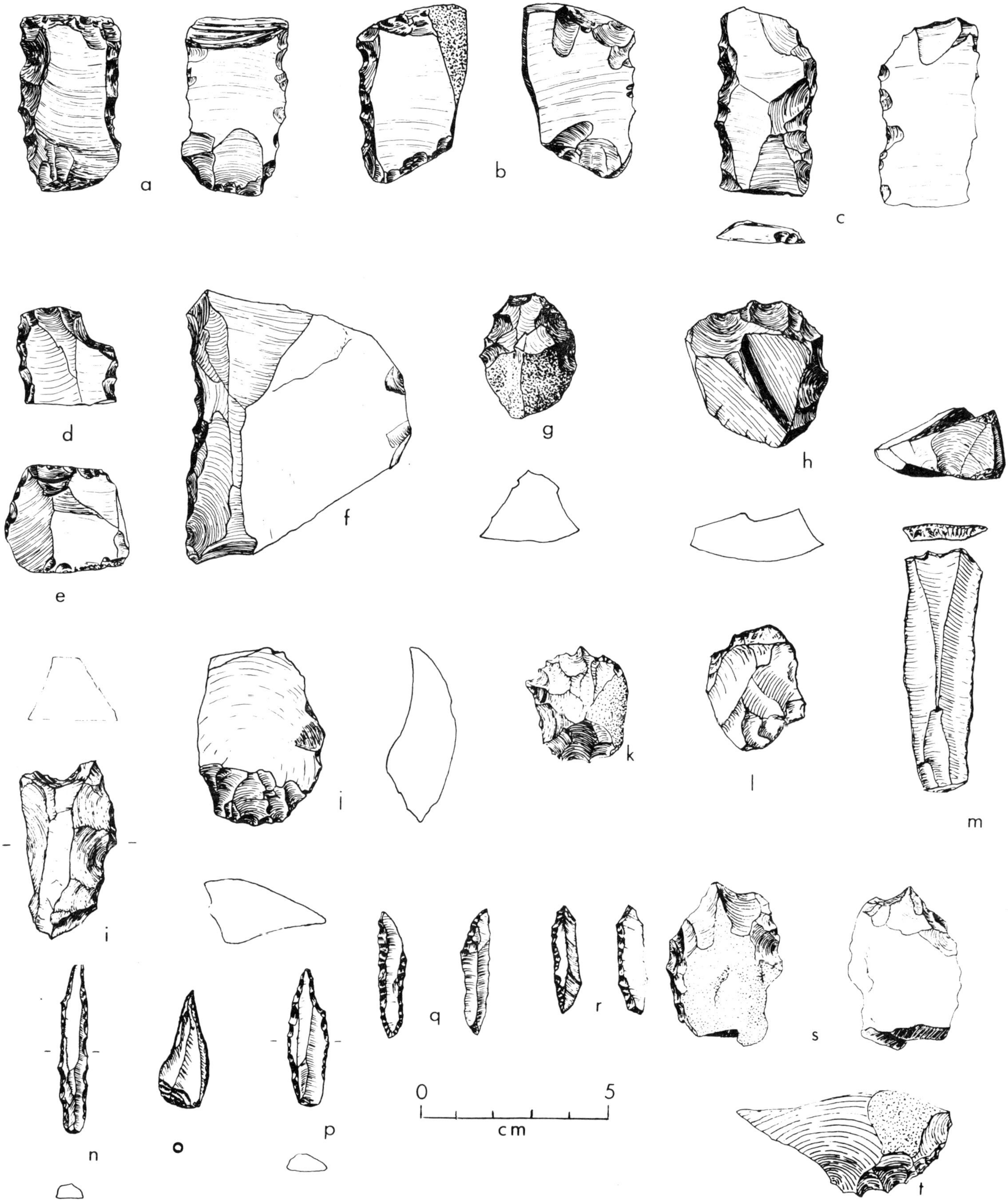

Figure 13. Side Scrapers, Steep Scrapers, End Scrapers, and Borers

a-f, Side scrapers, with snapped ends. g-k, Steep scrapers. l,m, End scrapers. n, Borer, double backed parallel sided. o,p, Borers, double backed triangular. q,r, Borers, double backed alternately backed on one side. s,t, Borers, simple.

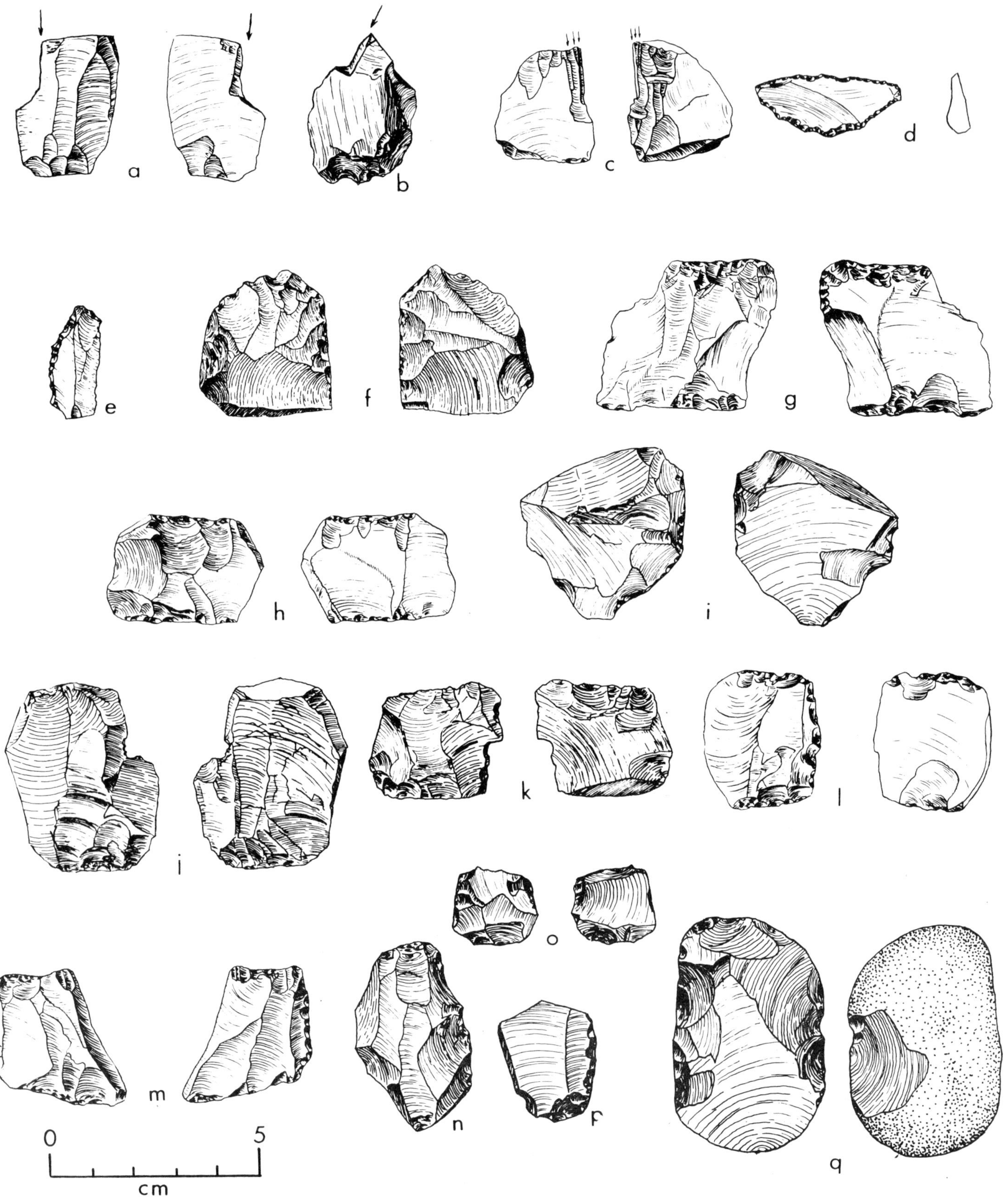

Figure 14. Burins, Backed Blade, Truncated Pièces, and Pieces Esquillées

a-c, Burins. d, Backed blade. e, Truncated backed blades. f, Pièce esquillée, with one edge battered. g-m, Pìeces esquillées, with two opposite edges battered. n, Pièce esquillée, with two adjacent edges battered. o-q, Pièces esquillées, with three edges battered.

Figure 15. Abraders, Pecking Stones, Rubbers, Pendants, Punctated Stone, Bead, Disc, and Incised Stone

a,b, Pebble abrader. c, Partly pecked abrader. d, Simple pecking stone. e, Elongate pebble pecking stone. f, Pecking stone-chopper. g, Pecking stone-rubber. h-j, Facetted rubbers. k-m, Pendants. n, Bead. o, Disc. p, Incised stone.

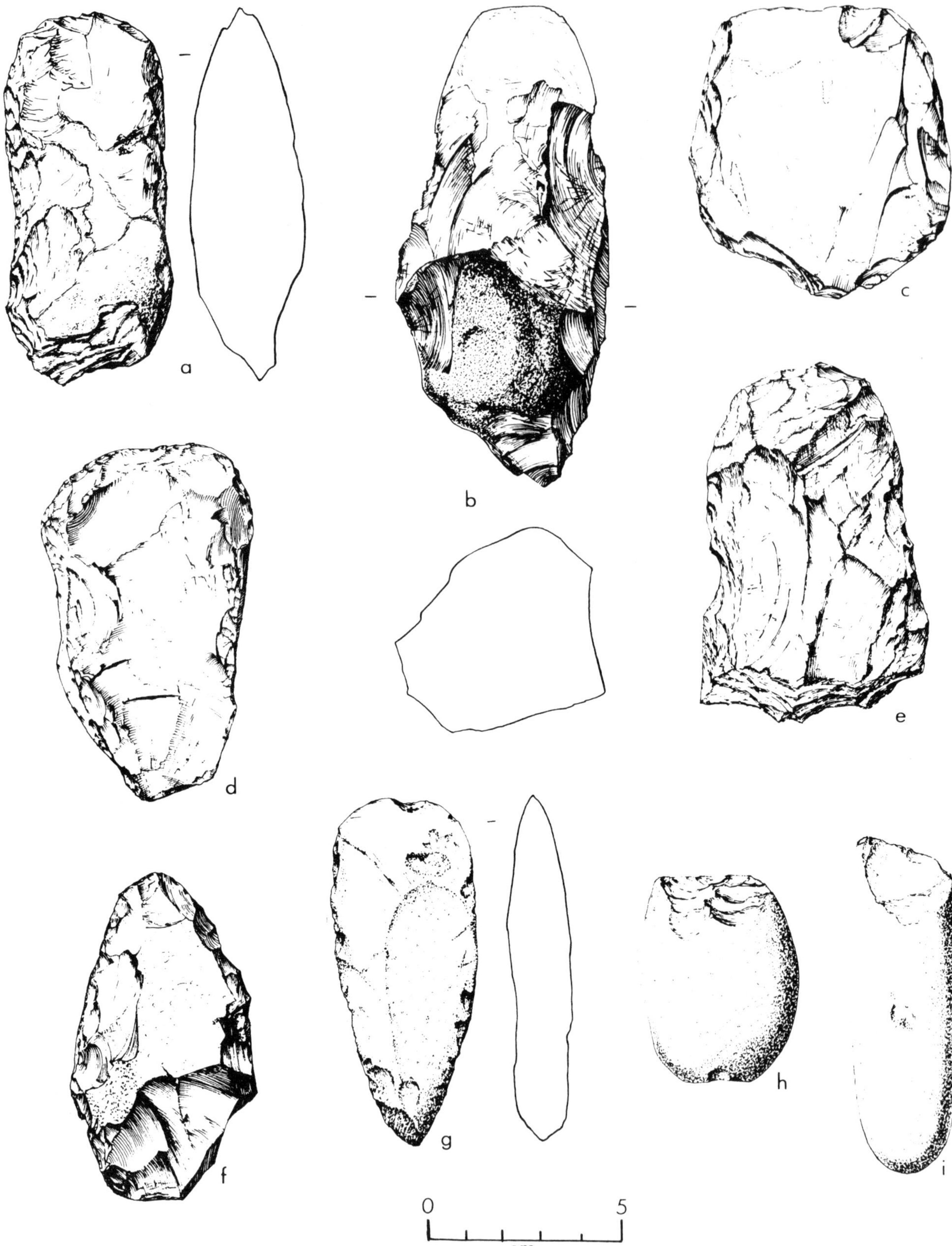

Figure 16. Celts and Chisels
(For Fig. 17 see after Fig. 1.)

a-c, Chipped celts with polished bits. d-f, Chipped celts with chipped bits. g, Allover smoothed polished celts. h,i, Chisels.

PLATES

a b c d

Plate 1. Views of Zawi Chemi Shanidar

a, Modern Shanidar village with Zawi Chemi Shanidar in the background. b, Excavation view at Zawi Chemi Shanidar. c, Northeast Wall, Cut 1, d, Portion of Northeast Wall, Cut 2, showing pit at base of Layer B.

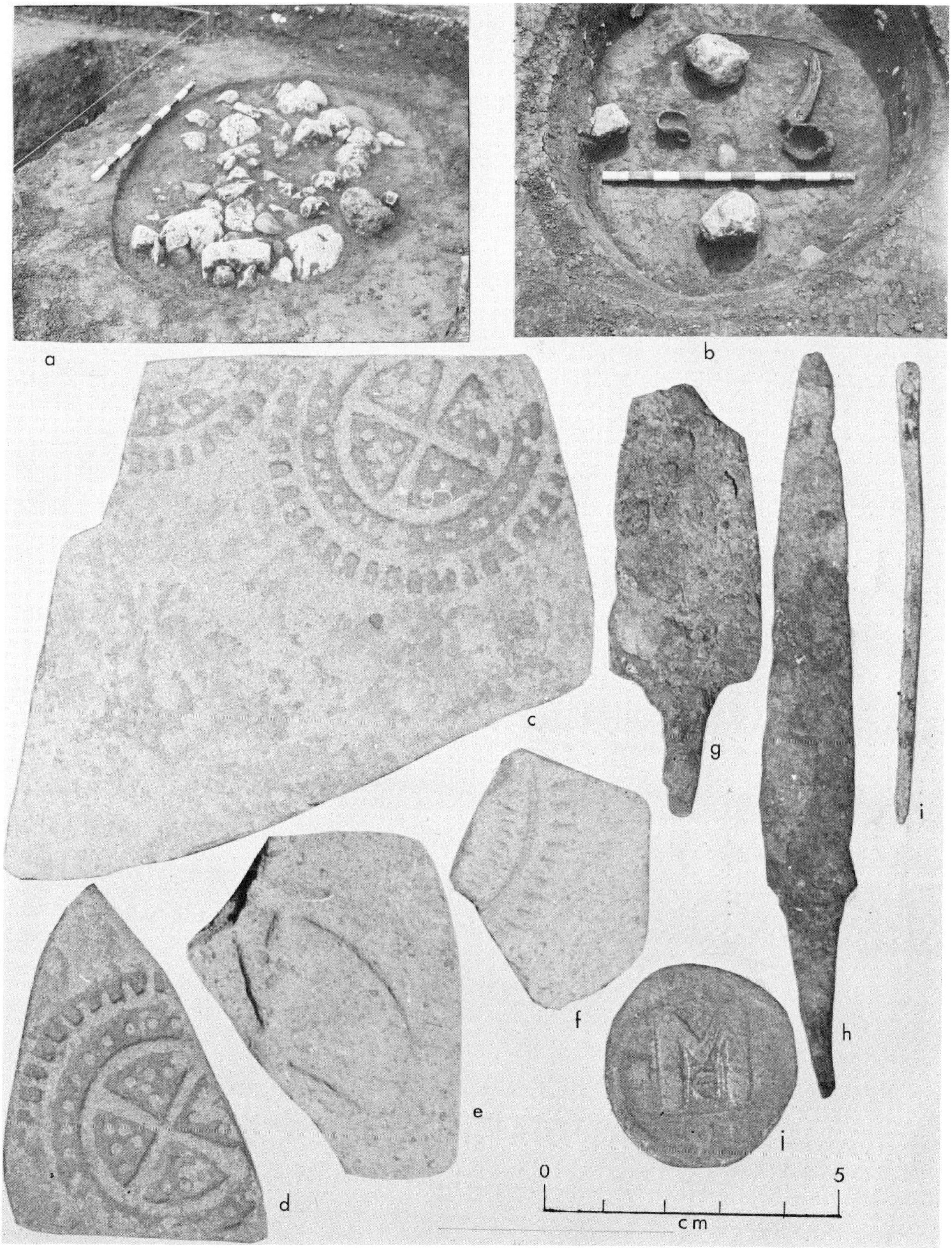

Plate 2. Features and Artifacts from Layer A

a,b, Pits. c-f, "Christian Ware". g,h, Spear points. i, needle. j, coin.

a

b

c

d

Plate 3. Structure I, Modern Animal Shelter, Modern Flood Plain Agriculture at Shanidar Village

a,b, Structure I, Cut 1. c, Modern animal shelter at Shanidar village. d, Modern flood plain agriculture at Shanidar village, along the Greater Zab river.

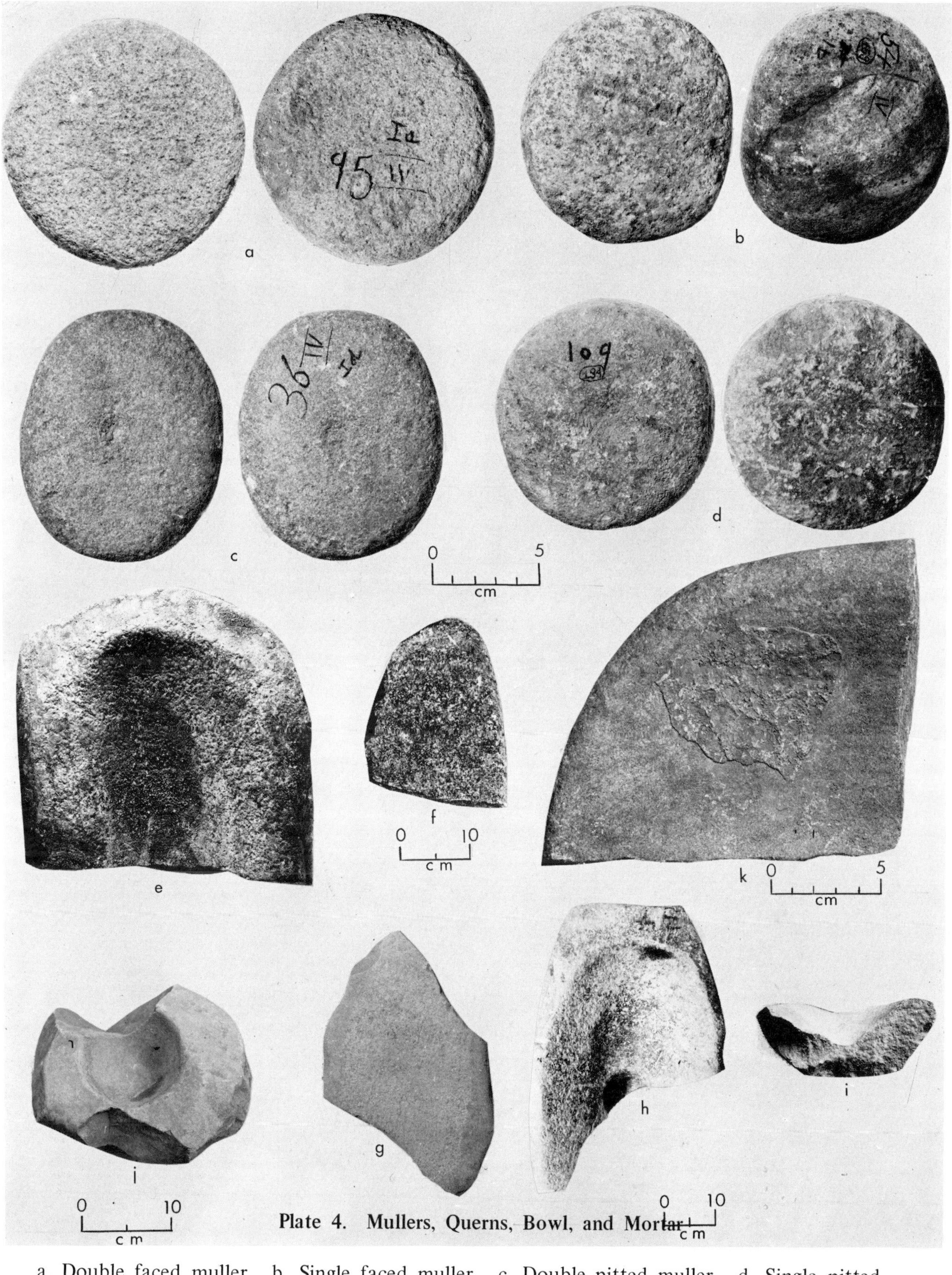

Plate 4. Mullers, Querns, Bowl, and Mortar

a, Double faced muller. b, Single faced muller. c, Double pitted muller. d, Single pitted muller. e, Trough quern. f,g, Flat querns. h,i, Combination quern-mortars. j, Mortar. k, Bowl.

V

Plate 5. Abraders, Pounder, and Hammerstones

a,b, Pebble abraders. c, Large pebble abrader. d, Partly pecked abrader. e, Pecked abrader. f, Combination pebble abrader-pecking stone. g, pounder. h-j, Simple hammerstones. k, Single pitted hammerstone. l, Double pitted hammerstone. m-q, Greenstone hammerstones.

Plate 6. Pecking Stone, Rubbers, Ring, Cupped Stone Shaped Slab, and Grooved Stones

a,b, Simple pecking stones. c, Elongate pebble pecking stone. d, Pecking stone-chopper. e, Pecking stone-rubber. f-l, Facetted rubbers. m, Simple rubber. n, Ring. o, Cupped stone. p, Shaped slab. q-u, Grooved stones.

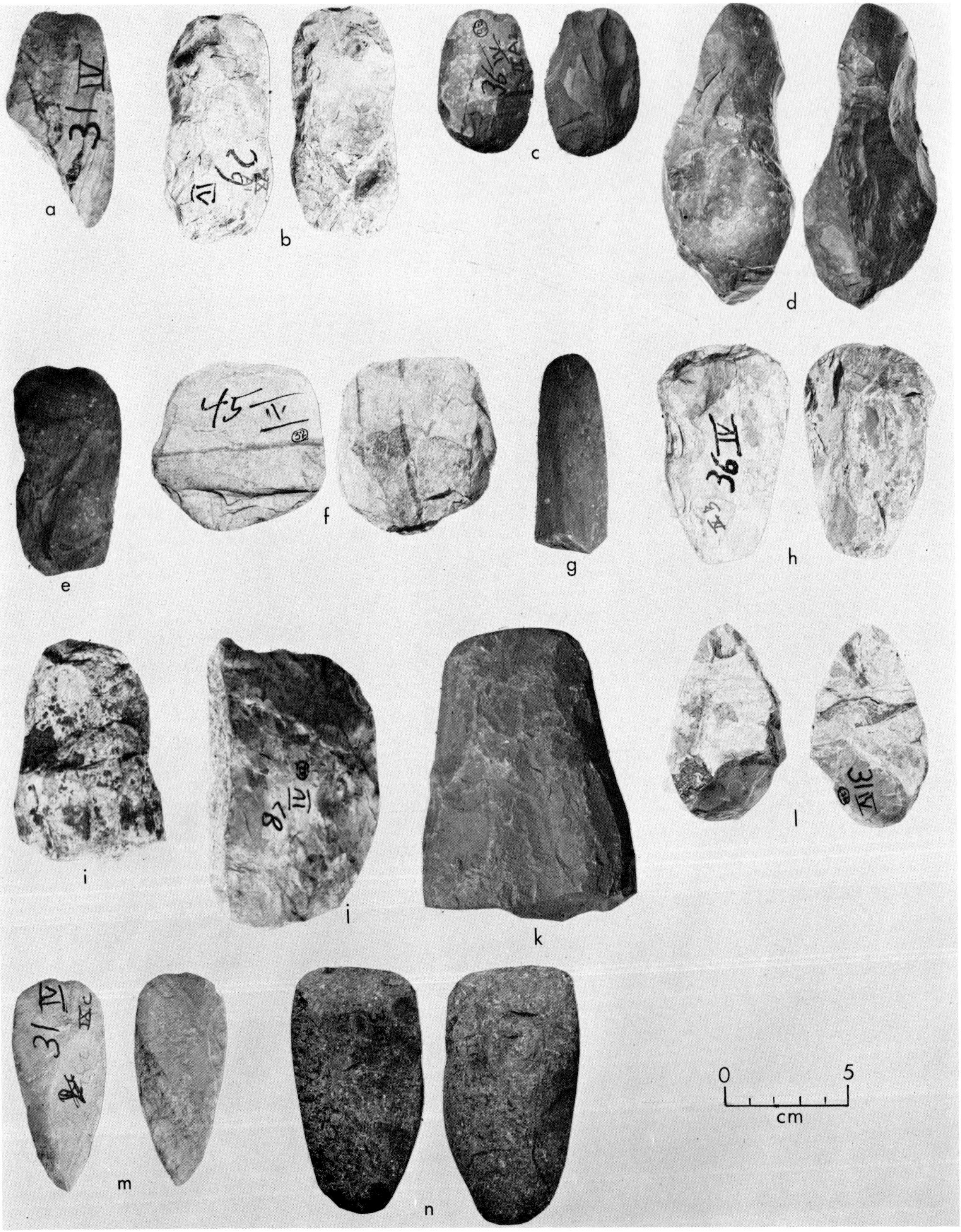

Plate 7. Celts

a-g, Chipped celts with polished bits. h-l, Chipped celts with chipped bits. m,n, Allover smoothed/polished celts.

Plate 8. Pendants, Beads, Discs, Fossils, and Other Small Miscellany

a-j, Pendants. k-n, Beads. o-q, Discs. r, Engraved stone. s,t, Taconite pebbles. u,v, Invertebrate fossils.

Plate 9. Choppers, Spall Tools, Spall Core, Chisels, and Flake Knife

a-i, Choppers. j-o, Spall tools. p, Spall core. q,r, Chisels. s, Flake knife.

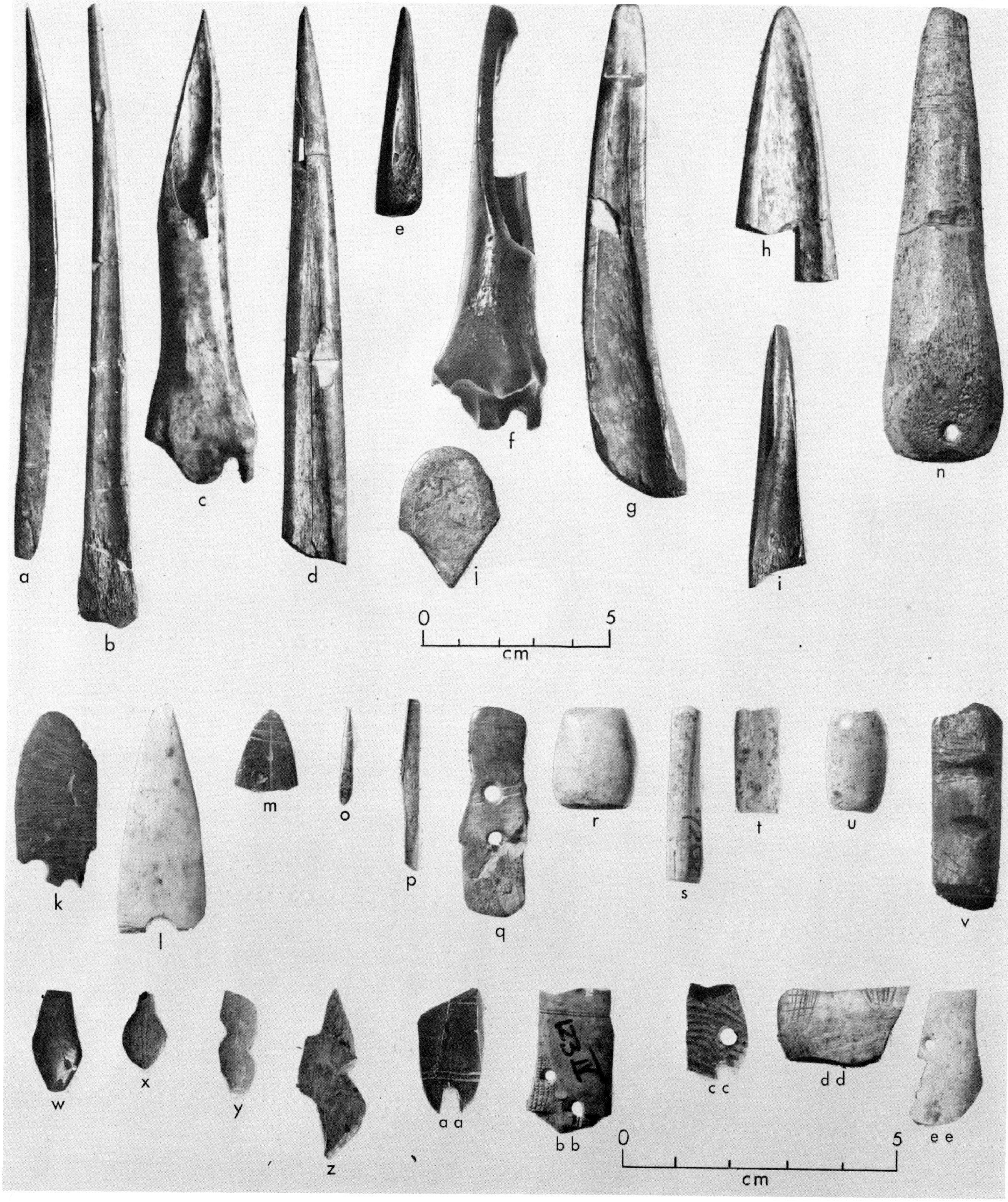

Plate 10. Bone Objects

a-e, Awls. f-i, Tools with polished, non-piercing ends. j, Spatula. k-m, Flat, pointed tools. n, Beveled ended tool. o, Tiny point. p. Cut bone piece. q, Double-holed winged object. r-v, Beads. w-ee, Decorated bone pieces.

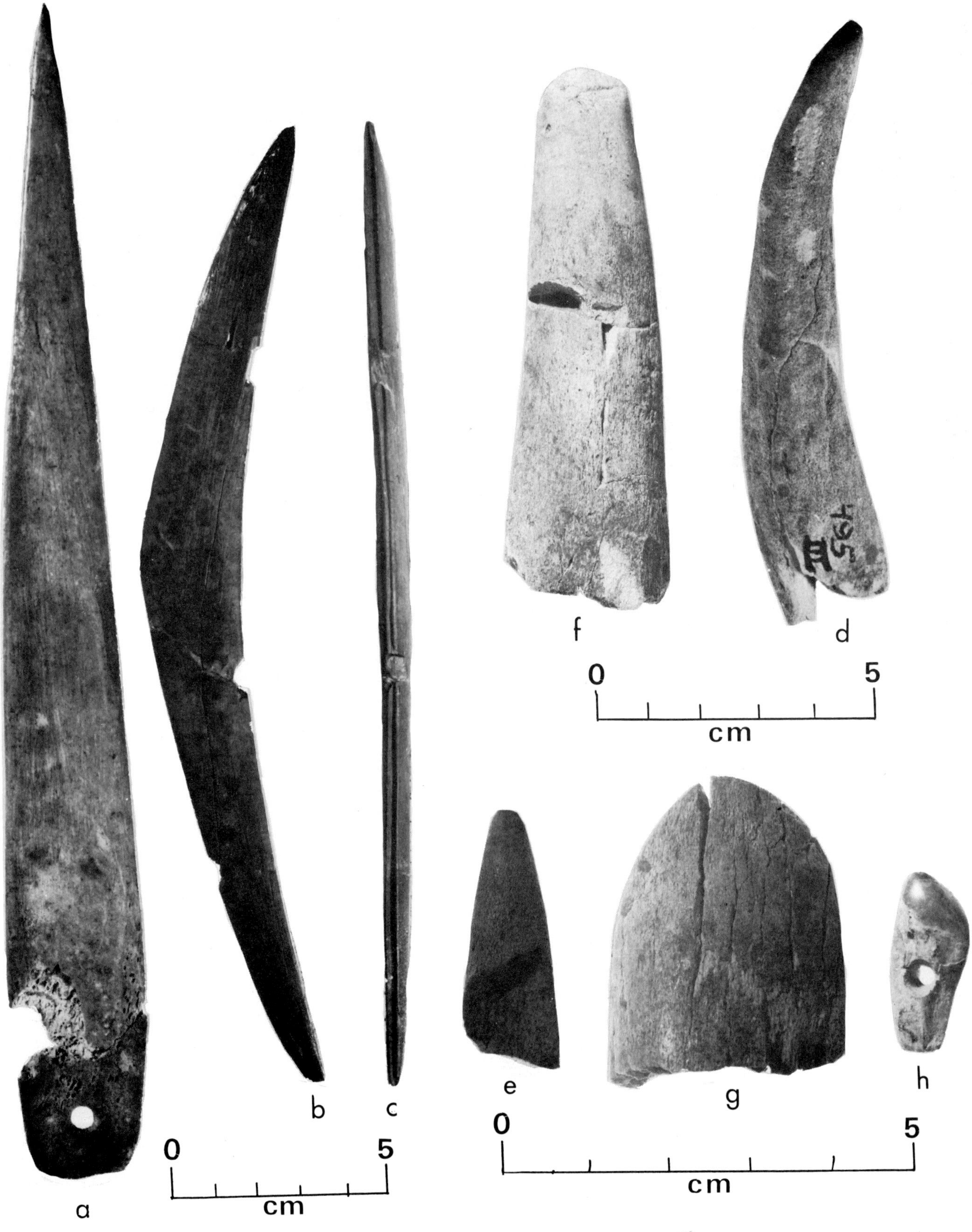

Plate 11. Bone, Antler, Horn, and Ivory Objects

a, Bone flat, pointed tool from Shanidar Cave. b,c, Bone haft. d-g, Antler and horn tools. h, Perforated animal tooth.